WOODEN SPOON
Wedding Cookbook

Carlisle Press
WALNUT CREEK

An Amish bride from Holmes County shares all her wedding recipes,
a look into her wedding, plus 350 of their extended family's favorites.

© Copyright February 2007 Carlisle Press

All rights reserved. No portion of this book may be reproduced by any means, electronic or mechanical, including photocopying, recording, or by any information storage retrieval system, without written permission of the copyright owner, except for the inclusion of brief quotations for a review.

ISBN *10 digit:* 1-933753-00-5
     13 digit: 9-781933-753003

    First Printing   September 2007 . 5M
    Second Printing   September 2011 . 5M

Cover photo by Jesse Miller
Cover design by Julia Hunsberger
Text design by Rhoda Miller
Text art by Aden Miller (Miriam's husband)
Printing by Carlisle Printing

2673 Township Road 421
Sugarcreek, OH 44681

Carlisle Press
WALNUT CREEK

A Note from
Miriam

On October 2, 2003, Aden and I were married. After having known each other for over three years, it was a dream come true. Compiling the recipes and recalling our wedding day together brought back many fond memories. We spent many hours together compiling *The Wooden Spoon Wedding Cookbook*. Two of my favorite hobbies are cooking and reading. If you enjoy these hobbies you'll love the work we've done here.

I use a lot of simple, tried and true recipes, but when I have time I also enjoy making something that's a bit more challenging, but looks nice. So whether you enjoy the easy-to-make or the more difficult recipes, you'll find something in *Wedding Cookbook* you want to try. Aden has a hearty appetite and is always willing to try my new recipes. So is our son Cristy who joined us on July 16, 2004. He has added some work and worry, but also lots and lots of joy to our lives. At 22 months old he is not a picky eater, always willing to sample Mom's new dishes and help himself to any cookies he finds! Our newest baby Ivan joined us on June 1, 2006. His boyish appetite is beginning to show.

In *Wedding Cookbook* my husband's family of eight sisters and five brothers all share their best recipes. Aden has four sisters younger than he, but he is the youngest of the six boys. His parents are Jacob and Esther Miller. Aden's aunts also shared recipes for this book. He has only one aunt on his mother's side, but six aunts and eight uncles on his father's side. So we don't take all the credit for the recipes in this book. A hearty thank-you goes to everyone who shared their recipes and stories.

You may find it interesting to know that in addition to being an accomplished woodworker, my husband is also an artist. He did all the pencil art for *Wedding Cookbook*.

Before you roll up your sleeves and get into the recipes, please take a moment to familiarize yourself with the symbols used in this book, found on page VI.

Miriam Miller

Wedding "Eck" Explanation

Throughout this book you will find the term "eck" used. This term in Pennsylvania Dutch literally means corner. For a traditional Amish wedding, though, it's the place where the bride and groom and their four witnesses eat two meals—dinner and supper. These tables are carefully arranged and decorated by the bride. On her wedding day hours of her own work surround her at the "eck." From the beautifully handmade wall decorations (behind the "eck") to the tables arranged to perfection, the "eck" is an expression of the bride's tastes. And yes, the tables are set in a corner with the bride and her witnesses on one side and the groom and his witnesses on the other.

Symbols used in Wedding Cookbook

This art accompanies those recipes used specifically by Miriam at her own wedding.

The recipes on screened pages are general recipes used at Amish weddings, contributed by Aden and Miriam's mothers, aunts and grandmothers.

With this symbol Miriam shares personal wedding memories of her and Aden's wedding day on October 2, 2003.

> *G*etting ready for a wedding starts nine months to a year ahead of time. We had to schedule to rent the things we needed at least nine months ahead or they were booked full. We rented a trailer with tables, 275 place settings besides a lot of di which are needed to prepare the food. Also lots of serving bowl

Enjoy an extra helping of Miriam's thoughts on married life in "love notes" in the margin.

2 t. sugar
¹/₂ c. Crisco or butter
²/₃ c. milk

r. Add rest of ingredients and mix. Roll and cut ungreased cookie sheet. Bake at 450° for 10-12 brown.

Mrs. John (Fannie) Miller

MILK BISCUITS

¹/₄ t. soda
6 T. shortening
³/₄ c. buttermilk or milk

t in shortening. Add milk. Many times our Sunday e gravy. Aden makes the biscuits while I make ong to get the meal on the table.

There is no surprise more magical than the surprise of being loved. It

1 c. shortening   3 c. flou
pinch of salt

Put ingredients in a bowl in order given. Beat a or 150 to 200 beats by spoon. Bake at 350° for

This is one of the first cakes I made when I was than once I made a mistake while making it, b ever flopped. I was 12 years old when my you Mom was at the birthing center I made thi was surprised when she got home, as I h without her help.

This wooden spoon highlights Miriam's special thoughts for the recipe.

LAZY WIFE CAKE

1¹/₂ c. pastry flour   3 T.

One of the first things I sewed for the wedding was six cushions. A cushion was put on each chair at the eck

Throughout the book Miriam shares personal notes about her and Aden's wedding day accompanied by artwork by Miriam's husband Aden.

Wooden Spoon Wedding Cookbook   VII

Miriam's First Dream Cookbook

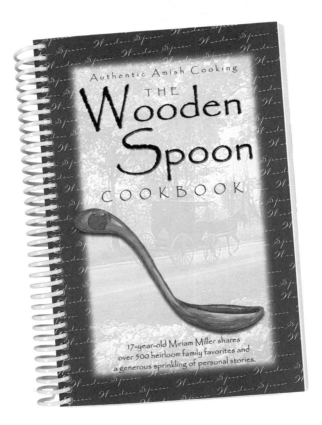

You may have met Miriam Miller for the first time when she was a single 17-year-old girl Amish girl who had a dream of compiling her own cookbook—*The Wooden Spoon*. Now in its eighth printing, *The Wooden Spoon* has become a favorite among people who enjoy Amish cooking all over the United States. It is available by calling 800.852.4482.

Table of Contents

Beverages 1

Breads, Rolls & Cereals 9

Salads & Salad Dressings 23

Meats & Main Dishes 33

Soups & Vegetables 69

Pies 79

Cakes, Cookies & Frostings 99

Desserts & Puddings 163

Candies & Snacks 193

Canning & Freezing 217

Miscellaneous 233

Index 241

X   *Wooden Spoon Wedding Cookbook*

Beverages

The punch was served, fresh as could be,
For it was made on our wedding day, you see!
My new sister-in-law made it after lunch;
Oh, how refreshing! A glass of ice-cold punch!

She took the recipe times six,
And then dumped and stirred and mixed.
Into the ice-house it was set, till it was cold,
And then the 7-Up was added, I was told.

My parents got the job of serving it,
And everyone thought that was really fit!
For Dad likes to talk to everyone,
Tell some jokes and have some fun!

The young folks each had their share,
Then we did what we thought was fair.
The older people and children got a taste,
Not even one drop went to waste.

*G*etting ready for a wedding starts nine months to a year ahead of time. We had to schedule to rent the things we needed at least nine months ahead or they were booked full. We rented a trailer with tables, 275 place settings besides a lot of dishes which are needed to prepare the food. Also lots of serving bowls. From another place, we rented four gas stoves to do the baking before the wedding and the cooking on the day of the wedding. And another must is the ice-house. That is a small insulated building, filled with shelves to store food, and a place to put your ice to keep the food cold.

Aden and Miriam
October 2, 2003

Holiday Punch

2 c. hot water
2 c. cold water
6 oz. strawberry Jell-O
1/2 gal. orange sherbet, softened

1 (2 liter) 7-Up
1 (46 oz.) orange juice
1 c. ReaLemon
1½ c. sugar

Pour hot water over Jell-O and stir until Jell-O is dissolved. Add cold water. Stir well. Add the rest of ingredients, adding 7-Up just before serving.

Since this punch is better the fresher it is, we waited to make it until the day of the wedding. We made six batches and had plenty, but the leftover was so good that we almost wished for more. When the young folks were eating their supper, my parents gave each person a small glass filled with punch. Of course, the bridal party got all they wanted.

Wedding Punch

6 pkg. Tropical Punch Kool-Aid
1 large can pineapple juice
1 large can grapefruit juice
2 (12 oz.) cans frozen lemonade
5 c. sugar
1 qt. ginger ale
12 qt. water

Mix all together. Add ginger ale just before serving. Serves 75 people.

Eli & Ella Stutzman

Punch

$2^1/_2$ pkg. orange Kool-Aid
$2^1/_2$ c. sugar
$2^1/_2$ gal. water
30 oz. frozen orange juice
$2^1/_2$ liters 7-Up
1 gal. orange sherbet

Can be made the day before the wedding. Add 7-Up and softened orange sherbet just before serving. Yield: 5 gallons.

Leroy & Lydia Miller

Mennonite Wine

1 (12 oz.) can frozen grape juice
1 (6 oz.) can frozen orange juice
1 c. white sugar
$^1/_4$ c. ReaLemon
2 liters ginger ale

Mix first four ingredients. Add enough water to suit your taste. Just before serving add ginger ale.

William & Elsie Miller

PUNCH

1 pkg. Tropical Punch Kool-Aid	2 liters Sprite
1 (6 oz.) can frozen orange juice	¹/₂ gal. orange sherbet
1 (46 oz.) can pineapple juice	

Mix Kool-Aid as directed. Add rest of ingredients. Ready to serve and enjoy.

PUNCH

1 can frozen orange juice	1 pkg. strawberry Kool-Aid
1 can frozen lemonade	7-Up
1 pkg. cherry Kool-Aid	

Mix each one as directed on can or package. Mix all together. Add 7-Up just before serving.

Mrs. John (Katie) Troyer

When I was a little girl, Mom had supper ready one evening and one of the neighbor men was still visiting with Dad. Mom told me, "As soon as he leaves, tell Dad that supper is ready." I went out and told Dad, "As soon as he leaves we want to eat supper." The neighbor got a big chuckle out of it. I don't think he ever forgot and I'm sure my family never did! *Miriam*

One of life's greatest treasures is the love that binds hearts together in friendship.

QUICK ROOT BEER

1 t. yeast
1 c. warm water

1¹/₂ c. sugar
4 t. root beer extract

In a gallon jar, dissolve yeast in 1 c. warm water. Add sugar, root beer extract and enough warm water to mix thoroughly until dissolved. Fill jar with water and set in a warm place, or sunlight, for several hours until strong enough; cool. Can be made in the morning and ready to drink by noon.

ICED TEA

4 qt. water
4 c. tea leaves

2 c. sugar

Pour boiling water over tea leaves. Let stand 15 minutes. Remove leaves. Do not add sugar until tea is cooled or it will turn brown.

Erma Miller

RHUBARB DRINK

4 qt. rhubarb juice
1 can frozen orange juice
1 can frozen lemonade
1 can frozen pineapple juice

7 qt. water
2 pkg. raspberry Kool-Aid
4 c. sugar

Fill an 8 qt. saucepan halfway with chopped rhubarb; fill with water. Bring to a boil; let stand 30 minutes. Drain. Add rest of ingredients. This can be canned.

HOT CHOCOLATE

1 c. chocolate syrup $1/2$ gal. milk
8 oz. marshmallow creme

Combine chocolate syrup and marshmallow creme thoroughly. Add hot milk and mix until well blended.

Mrs. Ivan A. Miller

A few months before our wedding I was at a restaurant and saw a waitress go by with someone's drink. What caught my eye was the pineapple and cherry that garnished the glass. I thought it's prettier than just a plain lemon slice, so I had the "eck" tablewaiters put one on our punch glasses.

NOTES

Breads, Rolls & Cereals

Rolls is what we chose for our wedding dinner,
With strawberry jam it seemed to be a winner!
The neighbor lady baked them with care;
She was even kind enough, her recipe to share.

Baked and delivered the day before,
Far better than the ones out of the store.
Four hundred dinner rolls was the count,
One on each plate, at the table, could be found.

Each roll in a sandwich bag was put,
And one on each plate if you could.
Our aim was to keep them from getting stale,
And our method sure did not fail!

For every roll was fresh as could be,
By the look on each face, you could see!
A smile on their face as they took a bite,
These rolls were made just right!

Aden and Miriam
October 2, 2003

Quick Buns

1 1/2 c. milk, scalded
1 c. cold water
2 T. yeast
2 eggs

2 T. shortening
3/4 c. white sugar
1 t. salt
7 c. flour

Put sugar, salt and shortening in a bowl; pour milk over it; stir until shortening is melted. Add cold water; add yeast. When yeast is bubbly add eggs and flour. Let rise until double in size; shape and let rise again. Bake at 325° for 25 minutes. Note: 2 c. wheat flour can be used instead of all white.

One of our neighbors bakes bread and dinner rolls for churches and weddings, so we ordered 400 dinner rolls from her. We picked them up the evening before the wedding. The day of the wedding my youngest sisters and Aden's youngest sister put the dinner rolls in sandwich bags and put one on each plate.

MOM'S HOMEMADE BREAD

$^1/_2$ c. lukewarm water
$^1/_2$ T. yeast
$^1/_4$ t. brown sugar
$^1/_4$ c. white sugar

$^1/_8$ c. vegetable oil
$^1/_4$ t. salt
1 c. warm water
flour

In a small bowl mix $^1/_2$ c. lukewarm water, yeast and brown sugar. In a large bowl mix white sugar, salt, vegetable oil and 1 c. warm water. Add 1 c. flour and beat well. Add yeast mixture. Add $^3/_4$ c. flour. Keep adding flour, a little at a time, beating well after each addition. When dough gets too stiff to beat, use hands to work in enough flour to make a soft dough. Grease hands occasionally. Grease bowl; turn dough upside down. Cover; let rise in a warm place. Knead three times at 45-minute intervals. Form into loaves; let rise until double in size. Bake at 400° for 20 minutes. Yield: 2 loaves.

GRANNY BREAD

$2^1/_2$ T. yeast
1 t. sugar
$^1/_2$ c. lukewarm water
2 c. warm water
$^1/_2$ c. white sugar

1 T. salt
$^1/_2$ c. vegetable oil
$^3/_4$ c. oatmeal
$^3/_4$ c. wheat flour
6-7 c. bread flour

Dissolve yeast and sugar in lukewarm water. Let stand 10 minutes. Mix all ingredients together. Knead 10 minutes. Let rise in warm place until double. Punch down and let rise again. Shape into loaves. Let rise. Bake at 350° for 30 minutes. Yield: 3 loaves.

Erma Miller

One of the first things I sewed for the wedding was six cushions. A cushion was put on each chair at the eck so we had soft seats since we did a lot of sitting that day. The pattern is called Bow Tie and the colors I used was dark blue, light blue and white.

WHITE BREAD

³/₄ c. white sugar	2 c. boiling water
³/₄ c. brown sugar	4 c. warm water
1¹/₂ c. flour	4 T. yeast
2 T. salt	1¹/₂ c. oil

Mix first 5 ingredients together. Then add the rest and add Thesco flour until dough is right. Let rise for 20 minutes, then knead it down. Let rise another ¹/₂ hour, then put in pans and let rise a little before you bake them. Bake at 350° for 20 to 30 minutes.

Mrs. Andy (Lizzie) Miller

BROWN BREAD

¹/₃ c. brown sugar	2¹/₄ c. hot water
¹/₃ c. honey	2¹/₄ c. cold water
1¹/₂ T. salt	3 T. yeast
1 c. wheat flour	1¹/₈ c. vegetable oil

Mix first 5 ingredients. Stir, then add cold water and yeast. Let rise until bubbly; add oil. Add enough flour to make a soft dough. Knead every 15 minutes for an hour. Form into loaves and bake at 350° for 30-35 minutes.

Rebecca Yoder

tips and hints

WHEN BAKING BREAD DO NOT WASH THE PANS EACH
TIME. THIS WILL KEEP THE BREAD FROM STICKING TO
THE PAN AS IT IS STILL GREASY.

TWO-HOUR BUNS

1 $1/2$ T. yeast
1 c. warm water
$1/4$ c. sugar
1 egg

1 T. shortening
$1/2$ t. salt
$31/2$ c. bread flour

Beat first 4 ingredients until foamy. Add shortening, salt and flour. Mix and knead just enough to blend well. Let rise until double in size, shape into buns, let rise again and bake at 400° for 15-20 minutes. These can be made in 2 hours.

Emma Miller

BROWN -N- SERVE BUNS

10-11 c. flour
$1/2$ c. sugar
4 t. salt
2 T. yeast

$11/2$ c. milk
$11/2$ c. water
$1/2$ c. shortening

In a large bowl, mix 3 c. flour, sugar, salt and yeast. Combine milk, water and shortening in saucepan; heat until very warm. Gradually add to dry ingredients and beat 2 minutes. Add 2 c. flour and again beat 2 minutes. Add 2 more c. flour and beat 2 more minutes. Stir in enough flour to make a soft dough; knead until smooth. Let rise until double. Divide into 4 equal pieces. Divide each piece into 12 pieces; shape each piece into a ball. Put into greased muffin cups or cake pans. Let rise until almost double. Bake at 275° for 20-25 minutes or until buns just start to change color. When cool, wrap in plastic bags and refrigerate up to 1 week. Before serving place on ungreased baking sheet. Bake at 400° for 10-12 minutes or until golden brown. Yield: 4 dozen buns.

Mrs. John (Katie) Troyer

BISCUITS

2 c. all-purpose flour
1/2 t. salt
4 t. baking powder
1/2 t. cream of tartar

2 t. sugar
1/2 c. Crisco or butter
2/3 c. milk

Cut shortening into flour. Add rest of ingredients and mix. Roll and cut or just drop them on an ungreased cookie sheet. Bake at 450° for 10-12 minutes or until lightly brown.

Mrs. John (Fannie) Miller

EASY BUTTERMILK BISCUITS

2 c. flour
2 t. baking powder
1 t. salt

1/4 t. soda
6 T. shortening
3/4 c. buttermilk or milk

Mix dry ingredients; cut in shortening. Add milk. Many times our Sunday dinner is biscuits and sausage gravy. Aden makes the biscuits while I make the gravy, so it doesn't take long to get the meal on the table.

BISCUITS A LA NANCY

4 c. flour
4 T. sugar
2 heaping T. sour cream
4 t. baking powder

1 t. soda
2/3 c. shortening
1 1/3 c. milk or buttermilk

Cut shortening into dry ingredients. Add milk and sour cream. Knead 25 times. Drop onto cookie sheet. Bake at 425° for 10 minutes. Can also be used for pizza dough.

There is no surprise more divine than the surprise of being loved. It is the finger of God on our shoulder.

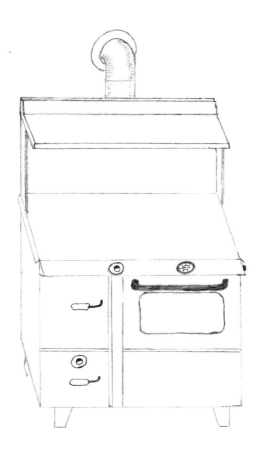

This is the stove where all our food is cooked and our goodies are baked during the winter. It also heats our house, though we do have a hard coal stove in the basement, which also helps heat the main floor. We have a clear gas stove that we use for cooking during the summer.

SWEET POTATO BISCUITS

1 1/2 c. mashed sweet potato
2 1/2 c. flour
2/3 c. sugar

2 T. baking powder
1/2 t. salt
1/3 c. oil

Mix everything together. It will be very dry. Use a tiny bit of flour to roll them out to ½" thick. Bake at 400° for 10-12 minutes until lightly brown. Can use butternut squash or pumpkin instead of sweet potato.

Mrs. Ervin (Mary) Byler

ROLLS

4 c. warm water
1/2 c. white sugar
1/4 c. oil
4 T. yeast

2 T. salt
eggs
6-6 1/2 c. flour
6 c. donut mix

Put sugar, water and yeast into large bowl. Let stand until bubbly. Then add oil, salt, eggs and the rest of the ingredients. Let rise until double. Roll out as for cinnamon rolls. Roll up. Put a thin slice in bottom of pan; next add a drop of cream cheese. Spread a thin layer of raspberry or any fruit filling (from a tube) on top of cream cheese. Top with a thin layer of rolls. Looks like a sandwich cookie. Let rise. Bake at 350° for 15-20 minutes. Ice with your favorite icing.

Mrs. Dan (Emma) Miller

OATMEAL ROLLS

2 c. warm water	2 T. yeast
$^1/_2$ c. white sugar	3 t. salt
6 T. vegetable oil	2 eggs, beaten
1 c. oatmeal	4-6 c. flour

Mix all together; let rise two hours. Shape into rolls and put into pans. Spread cinnamon, brown sugar and melted butter on the dough after it is rolled out. Let rise 45 minutes. Bake at 350° for about 30 minutes. Ice with your favorite icing. (The oatmeal cannot be tasted, but it keeps the rolls very soft.)

Barbara Miller

BEST CINNAMON ROLLS

2 T. yeast	1 t. salt
1 box yellow cake mix	melted butter
5 c. flour	brown sugar
3 eggs	cinnamon
$^1/_3$ c. oil	

Dissolve yeast in $2^1/_2$ c. water for 3 minutes. Add cake mix, 1 c. flour, eggs, oil and salt. Beat until bubbly. Add remaining flour to make a soft dough. Let rise until double. Roll and spread with melted butter, sugar and cinnamon. Roll up, stretch and cut. Place in pan and spread with butterscotch sauce. Bake for 25-30 minutes in a 350° oven. Immediately turn upside down on a tray so sauce is on top. Spread with favorite icing.

Butterscotch Sauce:

$^1/_3$ c. butter	1 T. corn syrup
$^1/_2$ c. brown sugar	$^1/_2$ c. nuts

Put first 3 ingredients in a saucepan and heat until boiling. Pour in pan and sprinkle with nuts.

Mrs. Uriah (Sevilla) Yoder

SOUR CREAM ROLLS

1 T. yeast	1 t. salt
$^1/_4$ c. warm water	$^1/_2$ c. sour cream
$^1/_4$ c. sugar	2 eggs, beaten
6 T. butter	$2^3/_4$ c. flour

Icing:

$^1/_4$ c. butter, softened	$^1/_2$ c. brown sugar
$^3/_4$ c. sour cream	

Knead like bread dough and let rise for two hours, covered. Knead dough
and divide in half. Roll each part into a 12" circle. Brush with melted butter. Top with mixture of 1 c. brown sugar, 1 t. cinnamon and chopped nuts.
Cut into 12 pie wedges. Roll from wide end to point. Put in jelly roll pan
and let rise. Bake at 350° for 25-30 minutes. Spread icing over rolls when
they come out of oven.

Mrs. Jonas D.A. (Edna) Miller

RASPBERRY-CREAM CHEESE ROLLS

2 c. warm water	2 eggs, beaten
$^1/_2$ c. white sugar	4-6 c. flour
$^1/_3$ c. vegetable oil	$^1/_2$ tube cream cheese filling
1 c. oatmeal	$^1/_2$ tube raspberry filling or any
2 T. yeast	fruit filling desired
3 t. salt	

Mix first 8 ingredients together. Let rise for two hours. Shape into rolls and
put into pans. I usually spread melted butter and cinnamon on when I roll
them. Using a scissors cut slits in top of rolls and fill with cream cheese
and raspberry filling. Let rise until double. Bake at 350° until nice and
brown, about 30 minutes. Frost with your favorite frosting.

Mrs. Levi (Mary) Miller

CINNAMON TWISTS

1 T. yeast	1¹/₂ t. salt
³/₄ c. warm water, divided	¹/₂ c. warm milk
4-4¹/₂ c. flour	¹/₄ c. butter, softened
¹/₄ c. sugar	1 egg

Filling:

¹/₄ c. butter, melted	4 t. cinnamon
¹/₂ c. packed brown sugar	

In a large mixing bowl dissolve yeast in ¹/₄ c. warm water. Add remaining ingredients. Turn onto a floured board; knead until smooth and elastic. Place into a greased bowl, turning once to grease top. Cover and let rise in a warm place (approximately 1 hour) until doubled. Punch down. Roll into a 16" x 12" rectangle. Brush with butter. Combine sugar and cinnamon; sprinkle over butter. Let dough rest for six minutes. Cut lengthwise into three 16" x 4" strips. Cut each strip into sixteen 4" x 1" pieces. Twist and place on greased cookie sheets. Cover and let rise until doubled. Bake at 350° for 15 minutes.

CEREAL

2 c. brown sugar	2 t. soda
10 heaping c. quick oats	1 c. nuts
2 c. wheat flour	1 c. coconut
1 pkg. graham crackers, crumbled	1 lb. butter, melted
1 t. salt	small butterscotch chips

Mix first eight ingredients well, then add butter and mix again. Toast at 300° for 1 hour, stirring every 15 minutes. When cool add butterscotch chips.

Emma Miller

CEREAL

8 c. quick oats	2 t. baking soda
2 c. brown sugar	1¹/₂ c. butter, melted
2 c. coconut	2 c. raisins
1-2 pkg. graham crackers	

Mix first five ingredients together. Add butter. Toast at 350° for 20-30 minutes. Add raisins. Cool; store in airtight containers.

Mrs. Ervin (Mary) Byler

GRANOLA CEREAL

8 c. quick oats	1¹/₂ t. soda
1 c. brown sugar	2 c. coconut
1 c. maple syrup	1 c. butter, melted
1 c. whole wheat flour	¹/₂ c. chocolate chips
1 t. salt	2 pkg. graham crackers

Mix first eight ingredients together. Toast slowly for one hour. Break graham crackers in pieces and add for last 15 minutes. When still warm add chocolate chips.

Mrs. John (Susan) Miller

UNCOOKED GRANOLA CEREAL

18 c. quick oats	4 c. raw sugar
9 c. wheat germ	1 t. salt
6 c. coconut	1¹/₂ c. butter

Mix and toast in oven at 300° to 350° for one hour. Makes a 13 qt. bowl almost full. Very good to eat with homemade grape nuts.

Mrs. Mahlon (Katie) Miller

Love makes everything lovely; hate concentrates itself on the one hated.

GRAPE NUTS

14 c. whole wheat flour
6 c. brown sugar
2 ¼ t. salt
1 T. soda

1 c. butter, melted
1 t. maple flavor
1 T. vanilla
1 ¼ qt. sour buttermilk

Put dry ingredients in bowl, except soda which should be added to milk. Add milk. Last add butter and flavorings. Mix well. Bake at 350°.

Mrs. Mahlon (Katie) Miller

The bridal party gets special food in special bowls. Our dinner rolls were served in this basket. The hot food was served in bowls that matched my china set and was garnished with parsley. Our water glasses had a lemon slice and we were the only ones to have ice cubes in our water.

Salads
Salad Dressings

Salad is a big favorite to me;
Almost any kind it can be.
But taco seems to be the best,
Because it's so different from all the rest!

Lettuce, hamburger and a sauce,
It has some zip; taco seasoning is the cause.
Add some chips, cheese and tomatoes,
For our wedding, this is what I chose!

Four thirteen-quart mixing bowls we had to fix;
Seven girls had to chop and mix.
In serving bowls on the table it was set;
The best salad ever, you can bet!

We were glad that most of it, the people ate,
For it gets soggy soon after it is made.
But still it has that great taco taste,
So we didn't let any go to waste!

Wooden Spoon Wedding Cookbook

The first thing we did when we got to my place after the ceremony was eat lunch. The men sang most of the afternoon. We were free to visit with the guests awhile before we passed out gifts to the people who had a part. Then we opened our gifts and soon it was time to eat supper, but we weren't hungry yet. After we had eaten we coupled up the young folks and they ate their supper while we ate our dessert—a sundae. They sang a few songs and all too soon everyone left for home and the day ended.

Aden and Miriam
October 2, 2003

Taco Salad

16 heads lettuce
12 (8 oz.) bags cheddar cheese, shredded
20 bags taco chips

8 boxes cherry tomatoes
26 lb. hamburger
onions, chopped fine
24 pkg. taco seasoning

Dressing:
6 c. salad dressing
3/4 c. ketchup
3/4 c. relish

$1^{2}/_{3}$ c. sugar
1/2 t. salt
2 T. taco seasoning

Mix hamburger and onions. Fry until no longer pink. Add taco seasoning. Cool. Chop lettuce; add hamburger, some cheese and chips. Just before serving add dressing. Put in serving bowls. Top with cheese, chips and tomatoes. This is enough to fill four 13 qt. bowls. We made six batches of dressing for this amount of salad, but had an ice cream pail full left over.

On our wedding day seven cousin girls made the salad. The hamburger was fried the day before and the dressing was mixed a few days in advance. We had also crushed the chips to make the job as simple as possible for them. We had the right amount of salad, but misjudged the amount of dressing and had a lot left over. So Mom canned some of it after the wedding. That way we got to eat wedding leftovers for a long time.

Aden and Miriam
October 2, 2003

Vegetable Pizza

4 c. flour
2 T. sugar
2 T. baking powder

2 t. salt
1 c. oleo
1 1/2 c. milk

Mix all ingredients. Divide into three 9" x 13" cake pans. Bake at 425° for 10 minutes. When cold pour some Ranch dressing over the top. Top with lettuce, carrots, radishes, cauliflower, celery, peppers, shredded cheese and bacon. Cut into pieces before topping with vegetables.

We baked 18 crusts on Monday when the neighbor ladies came to help. They were stored in plastic bags. Then after lunch the day of the wedding the tablewaiters poured the dressing on the crusts, chopped the vegetables and sprinkled cheese on top. We like this recipe as the crust is not very thick and not as sweet as some.

Cauliflower Broccoli Salad

30 heads cauliflower
15 heads broccoli

12 lb. grated cheese
15 lb. fried bacon

Dressing:
8 qt. mayonnaise or salad dressing
8 qt. sour cream
8 c. white sugar
8 pkg. Hidden Valley Ranch
    dressing mix

$^3/_4$ c. vinegar, or enough to suit
    your taste
salt to taste

Put cauliflower and broccoli through Salsa Master. Add cheese and bacon, saving some to put on top of serving bowls. Mix dressing ingredients. Pour over cauliflower broccoli mixture. This makes enough to fill four 13 qt. mixing bowls.

Jonas and Sara Miller

POTATO SALAD

12 c. potatoes, cooked
1 small onion

1 dozen eggs, boiled
$1^1/_2$ c. celery, chopped fine

Dressing:
3 c. salad dressing
2 T. vinegar
3 t. salt

$2^1/_2$ c. white sugar
$^1/_2$ c. milk
4 T. mustard

Put potatoes and eggs through Salad Master. Add rest of ingredients.

Mrs. Jacob (Esther) Miller

TACO SALAD

1 medium head lettuce, chopped
1 lb. hamburger
8 oz. cheese, coarsely grated
1 small can kidney beans

1 large onion, chopped
4 medium tomatoes, diced
1 pkg. taco flavored chips
1 pkg. taco seasoning

Dressing:
8 oz. Thousand Island, French
    or Russian dressing
$^1/_3$ c. sugar

1 T. taco seasoning
1 T. taco sauce

Brown hamburger; add taco seasoning, reserving 1 T. for dressing. Select a large salad bowl, allowing enough room to toss at serving time. Layer ingredients in bowl, starting with lettuce and ending with cheese. Cover and refrigerate. At serving time toss salad with dressing and taco chips.

Miriam Miller

VEGETABLE PIZZA

2 pkg. crescent rolls
1 head cauliflower, cut up fine
2 bunches broccoli, cut up fine

tomatoes and peppers, optional
8 oz. cheddar cheese

Filling:
8 oz. cream cheese, softened
16 oz. sour cream

1 pkg. Hidden Valley Ranch dressing
$1^1/_2$ c. Miracle Whip

Bake crescent rolls on large cookie sheet with sides at 350° for 10 minutes. Cool. Mix the filling ingredients well. Spread on crust. Cut into pieces the size you want, then add the vegetables. It is easier to cut before vegetables are added.

Mrs. David D. (Emma) Miller

VEGETABLE PIZZA

1/4 c. oleo	1/4 c. warm water
2 T. sugar	1 egg, beaten
1/4 c. boiling water	1 1/2 c. flour
1 pkg. yeast	1 t. salt

Mix together oleo, sugar and boiling water. Melt oleo, then cool to lukewarm. Sprinkle 1 pkg. yeast in 1/4 c. warm water and stir till dissolved. Add egg and yeast mixture to sugar mixture. Add flour and salt. Spread on cookie sheet and bake at 350° till light brown.

About six months before the wedding, we started saving all our tin cans that were the right size. I put ivy contact paper over each one. They were set on the table and filled with celery sticks on our wedding day. We put a little water in the bottom of each can to keep the celery crisp.

A great marriage is not when the "perfect couple" comes together. It is when an imperfect couple learns to enjoy their differences.

2 (8 oz.) pkg. cream cheese	lettuce, cauliflower, broccoli,
1 c. salad dressing	tomatoes, carrots, peppers,
1 pkg. Ranch dressing powder	bacon, cheese

Mix together cream cheese, salad dressing and Ranch dressing. Spread on crust after it's baked. Top with chopped vegetables.

Mrs. Levi (Mary) Miller

SALAD DRESSING

1 t. salt	$^1/_2$ c. sugar
2 t. prepared mustard	2 T. flour
1$^1/_2$ c. water	1 egg, well beaten
4 T. vinegar	

Cook until thick. Remove from heat and add 2 T. butter. When cool add 1 c. salad dressing.

Emma Miller

L&K DRESSING

1 c. vegetable oil	1 c. sugar
1 c. salad dressing	$^1/_4$ c. vinegar
pinch of salt	1 c. chopped onion
$^1/_2$ t. mustard	

Mix in order given. Will keep a long time in refrigerator.

tips and hints

CARROTS WERE FIRST GROWN AS

MEDICINE, NOT FOOD.

SWEET -N- SOUR DRESSING

1 c. sugar
1 c. oil
2 heaping T. salad dressing
1 heaping T. mustard
$1/4$ c. vinegar

$1/4$ c. water
$1/4$ t. black pepper
1 t. salt
$1/4$ t. celery seed
chopped onions if desired

Mix sugar and oil, then it won't separate. Add other ingredients in order given and beat well. Keeps a long time in refrigerator.

Mrs. John (Katie) Troyer

tips and hints

IF YOUR LETTUCE DRESSING SEPARATES, BEAT IN MORE SALAD DRESSING UNTIL IT DOESN'T SEPARATE ANYMORE.

MRS. JOHN (KATIE) MILLER

To keep marriage brimming, with love in the loving cup, whenever you're wrong admit it, whenever you're right, shut up.

Most Amish homes have a china cabinet like this. Some girls get one from their parents and others don't. I got a sewing machine instead of a china cabinet. My uncle built this one for us. The top doors have glass so you can see the china set and the Corelle set, and the top shelf holds my special glass pieces. The bottom doors are a great storage space for some of my dishes.

Meats & Main Dishes

Mashed potatoes, gravy and dressing too—
A wedding without chicken wouldn't do.
Add a dinner roll and slice of cheese,
Some salad and celery, if you please.

However good the food may be,
Leave some room; there's dessert, you see!
A bowl of date pudding, layered so nice;
You'll only take a bit if you are wise.

A bowl of colorful fruit I see,
Two kinds of jelly rolls it will be!
Two kinds of pies to choose from,
A cup of coffee if you want some.

Don't leave the table just yet,
There's a candy basket coming, I'd dare bet!
Choose a piece or two, to suit your taste,
But eat all you get and do not waste!

Wooden Spoon Wedding Cookbook

The day after the wedding we started washing dishes at 5:00 a.m. We were done by noon. The witnesses helped us, which is expected. Usually the girls wash and the boys dry the dishes. Four of my friends were dishwashers the day of the wedding, but their job ended when the young folks ate, so that means we had all the supper dishes from the young folks. By 2:00 p.m. the tables, dishes and stoves were gone, so the shop looked big and empty. So many memories made in such a short time!

Aden and Miriam
October 2, 2003

Mashed Potatoes

150 lb. potatoes
2 lb. butter
8 (8 oz.) pkg. cream cheese
4 gal. milk

4 pt. cream
salt
2 lb. brown butter

Peel potatoes and divide into sixteen 6 qt. saucepans. When mashing them add to each saucepan: $1/4$ c. butter, 4 oz. cream cheese, $1/2$ c. cream and enough salt to taste. Drizzle with brown butter on each serving bowl.

We had ten women making mashed potatoes the day of the wedding. They peeled close to 150 lbs. potatoes, which filled sixteen 6 qt. saucepans. To each saucepan they added $1/4$ c. butter, 4 oz. cream cheese, $1/2$ c. cream and salt to taste. After dishing it out into serving bowls they drizzled brown butter over the top. The bowl that the wedding table got had a sprig of parsley. It must have been good as we didn't have much left over.

Aden and Miriam
October 2, 2003

Gravy

3 qt. chicken broth
$1/2$ lb. butter
$1/2$ c. chicken base
1 t. pepper

3 c. cornstarch
1 dozen egg yolks
water

Melt butter in 12 qt. saucepan. Add chicken broth and enough water to fill saucepan $3/4$ full. Use wire whisk to mix cornstarch and egg yolks with enough water to make a thin paste. Bring broth to a boil. Turn burner off. Stir paste into broth slowly, stirring all the time. Turn burner on again and bring to a boil again. Turn burner off as soon as it boils.

Grandma and two of my aunts had the job of making enough gravy for everyone to top their mashed potatoes and dressing with. They made two 12 qt. and one 6 qt. saucepans full. We had so much left over that Mom canned some after the wedding. It was much more simple to open a can of gravy than to make it.

Aden and Miriam
October 2, 2003

Dressing (or stuffing)

1 qt. potatoes
1 qt. carrots
1 qt. celery
1½ qt. chicken
onions
parsley
1 doz. eggs

2 T. salt
1 T. pepper
1 T. seasoned salt
2 T. chicken base
bread
milk

Add enough milk and bread to make a 13 qt. mixing bowl full. Season to your liking. We used around 4 gallons milk and 20 large loaves of white bread.

Before the wedding day we cut up and cooked all the vegetables and chicken. We cubed and toasted the bread about a week in advance. The day of the wedding Mom's five sisters made the dressing. They made five 13 qt. mixing bowls full. We didn't have enough ovens for all of it so they made some on top of the stove. There was enough left, so we warmed it up for the young folks for supper. Then we still had a little left over for the next day.

Aden and Miriam
October 2, 2003

Yummi-Setti

¾ lb. butter
6 cans cream of mushroom soup
8 qt. water
3 lb. medium Inn Maid noodles
2 T. chicken base
a little pepper
salt to taste
6 lb. fried hamburger
1 medium onion
1½ lb. Velveeta cheese

Fry hamburger and onion together. Brown butter in a 20 qt. stainless steel canner. Add soup and stir until smooth. Add water and bring to a boil. Now add the noodles and seasonings. Let come to a boil before adding hamburger. Bring to a boil again. Put lid on and let stand 1½ hours. Stir and add cheese. Serves 100 people.

A lot of people have noodles or Potluck Potatoes at their wedding for supper. I wanted something different and this is what I came up with. We made 2 canners full and had a nice amount left over.

Aden and Miriam
October 2, 2003

Meat Loaf

15 lb. hamburger
5 1/2 c. cracker crumbs
2 c. oatmeal
5 T. salt

2 1/2 t. pepper
10 eggs
7 1/2 c. water

Sauce:
2 c. ketchup
3/4 c. brown sugar

2 T. mustard

Mix dry ingredients. Add to hamburger, eggs and water. Press into a greased loaf pan. Bake at 350° until no longer pink. When almost done, spread sauce on top and cut into pieces.

To save time we mixed all the dry ingredients ahead of time and put them in a Zip-Lock bag. When they were ready to make the meat loaf, they put 15 lb. hamburger in a 13 qt. mixing bowl, then added the other ingredients. We had 75 lb. hamburger, but had a lot left over. The sauce we also made ahead of time. I don't know how many batches we made, but we had 3 qt. sauce.

Aden and Miriam
October 2, 2003

Chicken Crumbs

6 c. Flaky Crust flour
3 c. whole wheat flour
3 c. cornmeal
6 T. chicken seasoning

Mix together. Use to coat chicken before frying. Fry in butter and vegetable oil. We got 3 lb. butter and 12 (48 oz.) bottles of vegetable oil.

Six women were first to arrive on our wedding day. Their job was to fry 250 lb. chicken. We had 175 lb. legs and thighs and 75 lb. wedding cuts from Gerber's. They fried it out on the back porch and were almost done when the other people started arriving. We had lined 20 roasters with aluminum foil, and they filled them with fried chicken and put them in the ovens until it was tender. We had about three roasters of chicken left over, which was about right. Mom made the recipe for the crumbs and I haven't tasted any chicken that is better than hers. I lost track of how many batches of crumbs we made, but enough to fill three ice cream pails. It only took two pails then.

Aden and Miriam
October 2, 2003

Breakfast Casserole

3 c. cubed bread
3 c. diced ham, sausage or bacon
3 c. shredded cheese
chopped onion

6 eggs, beaten
1 T. flour
2 T. butter, melted
3 c. milk

Layer first four ingredients in order given in a greased 7" x 10" pan. Beat eggs and add rest of ingredients. Pour over layered ingredients. Refrigerate overnight. The next morning bake uncovered at 325° for 1 hour.

A few of these casseroles were made the day before our wedding. My aunt and cousins from Michigan plus the witnesses were all there for breakfast the morning of our wedding day, so it was handy to pop these casseroles in the oven that morning.

Potluck Potatoes

10 lb. potatoes
³/₄ c. butter, lightly browned
3-4 cans cream of chicken soup
4 t. salt
³/₄ t. pepper
1½ c. French onion dip

4-6 c. milk
½ box Velveeta cheese
2 c. longhorn cheese
4 c. crushed cornflakes
3 T. brown butter

Cook potatoes and cool. Put through Salad Master. Heat next eight ingredients until cheese is melted. Add to potatoes. Add brown butter to crushed cornflakes. After potatoes are in serving bowls, top with cornflakes. This recipe is enough to fill one Lifetime roaster.

Leroy & Lydia Miller

Meat Loaf

5 lb. hamburger
1 c. oatmeal
1¹/₂ c. cracker crumbs
2¹/₂ c. milk

6 t. salt
1 t. black pepper
4 eggs

Mix all together and bake at 375° until done. We had this meat loaf for all of our daughters' weddings. The children keep saying Mom's meat loaf is better than others'.

Mrs. Jacob (Esther) Miller, Mrs. Alvin (Ida) Miller

Noodles for Wedding

1 c. butter
2 large cans College Inn chicken
   broth
$^1/_2$ can chicken base

5$^1/_2$ lb. Inn Maid noodles
1 large can mushroom soup
1 lb. Velveeta cheese

Melt butter in 20 qt. canner until brown. Add broth and fill with water until $^3/_4$ full. Add chicken base; bring to a boil. Add noodles; bring to a boil again. Boil for 1 minute. Remove from heat; add soup and cheese. Let stand 1 hour. Serves 100 people.

Mrs. David D. (Emma) Miller

Chicken Crumbs

2 boxes Bisquick
5 lb. whole wheat flour
12 c. all-purpose flour
9 T. salt
4$^1/_2$ T. paprika

5 T. garlic salt
6 T. Accent
6 T. sugar
18 T. salt
3 T. black pepper

This is enough to fill three ice cream pails.

Mrs. Jacob D. (Esther) Miller

MEAT LOAF

10 lb. hamburger	$^{1}/_{2}$ T. black pepper
8 eggs	1 T. seasoned salt
5 c. milk	4 c. saltine crackers
1 c. water	1 c. rolled oats
3 T. salt	

Put $^{1}/_{4}$ c. water in each cake pan. Divide meat into pans. Bake at 350° until done. Serves 50 people.

Mrs. John D. (Katie) Miller

BARBECUED MEATBALLS

3 lb. hamburger	1 c. cracker crumbs
1 c. oatmeal	$^{1}/_{2}$ t. garlic powder
$^{1}/_{2}$ c. chopped onions	$^{1}/_{2}$ t. seasoned salt
2 eggs, beaten	$^{1}/_{2}$ t. pepper
12 oz. Carnation milk	

Sauce:

1 c. ketchup	$^{1}/_{4}$ c. brown sugar
$^{1}/_{4}$ c. vinegar (scant)	3 t. mustard
1 T. Worcestershire sauce	water (if you want thinner sauce)

Mix all meatball ingredients together and form into balls; place on baking sheet and brown approximately 20 minutes at 350°. Put in roaster. Combine sauce ingredients and pour over meatballs. Bake another 30-40 minutes, or you can just finish baking them on the baking sheet too. Yield: 4 dozen meatballs.

Mrs. David D. (Emma) Miller

MEATS & MAIN DISHES

MOCK HAM

1 lb. hot dogs	2 lb. hamburger
2 c. cracker crumbs	2 eggs

Glaze:

¹/₂ c. brown sugar	1 c. water
1 T. mustard	

Mix half of glaze with meat. Pour other half on top of meat. Bake at 350° for 1 hour.

Mrs. Jonas D.A. (Edna) Miller

CHICKEN BURGERS

16 lb. ground chicken	¹/₂ c. salt, scant
4 slices bread, crumbled	4 eggs
1 pack white crackers, crushed	1 t. black pepper, or to taste
1 c. quick oats	red pepper, optional
4 c. water	

Mix all ingredients together. Form into patties and fry on hot skillet. For canning you can put burgers in jars and add a little water to the jars. Cold pack for 2 hours. We like it better to pack raw in jars like hamburger. Pressure can at 10 lb. for 1¹/₂ hours or like any other raw meat. Slice and fry.

Mrs. John (Katie) Troyer, Mrs. Alvin (Ida) Miller

A faithful friend is a strong defense; and he that has found him has found a treasure.

Wooden Spoon Wedding Cookbook **45**

CHICKEN TURNOVERS

2 c. flour
$^3/_4$ c. milk
$^1/_4$ c. shortening

3 t. baking powder
$^1/_2$ t. salt

Mix all together and roll out.

Filling:

1 c. chicken, cooked and diced
1 c. grated cheese
3 T. mayonnaise

salt and pepper to taste
1 t. onion
$^1/_4$ c. chopped celery

Mix together and put filling inside dough and press together, forming half-moon pies. Bake at 400° for 15 minutes. Serve with chicken gravy.

Mrs. Eli (Ella) Stutzman

BILL'S SANDWICHES

1 lb. chipped ham, finely cut
$^1/_2$ lb. Velveeta cheese, cut in
   small pieces

2 hard-boiled eggs, chopped
2 T. salad dressing
onion to taste

Mix all ingredients together and put on 8 buns. Wrap in foil and heat.

tips and hints

THERE ARE MORE CHICKENS THAN

PEOPLE IN THE WORLD.

Wedding Gifts

Everyone who attends the wedding brings a gift. Some were wrapped in pretty paper and others were in gift bags. But many of them were wrapped in towels, and that way we could even use the wrap instead of throwing it away! We got around 40 towels, all sizes and colors. After we had eaten lunch, Aden and I and our witnesses got to open the gifts. Never before had I gotten so many gifts in one day. We had to buy several items after we moved, but we got most of the items at the wedding to start keeping house.

MEATS & MAIN DISHES

CORN DOGS

³/₄ c. yellow cornmeal
³/₄ c. self-rising flour
1 egg, beaten
²/₃ c. milk

10 small wooden sticks
10 hot dogs
oil for deep-fat frying

In a bowl combine cornmeal, flour and egg and mix well. Stir in milk to make a thick batter; let stand four minutes. Insert sticks into hot dogs; dip into batter. Heat oil to 375°. Fry corn dogs approximately 5-6 minutes until golden brown. Drain on paper towel. As a substitute for self-rising flour, place 1 t. baking powder and ¹/₄ t. salt in a measuring cup. Add enough all-purpose flour to equal ³/₄ cup.

Mrs. John (Fannie) Miller

POTATO CASSEROLE

9 c. potatoes
1¹/₂ c. ham or meat of your choice, cut in squares

Sauce:
1¹/₂ T. melted butter
1 can mushroom soup
¹/₂ c. salad dressing or sour cream
1¹/₄ c. milk
¹/₂ t. salt

¹/₄ t. onion salt
¹/₂ t. Lawry's salt
1 t. black pepper, scant
Velveeta cheese, as desired

Cook potatoes with salt until nearly tender. Heat sauce ingredients together, adding Velveeta last. Heat until melted. Add 1 T. sour cream and onion powder when using salad dressing. Put in layers in small roaster or casserole dish. Add a little milk if too thick. Top with 1 c. crushed cornflakes mixed with 2 T. melted butter. Bake at 350° for 45 minutes or until hot.

Mrs. John (Katie) Troyer

Wooden Spoon Wedding Cookbook

POTATO AND EGG CASSEROLE

4 strips bacon
4 c. diced potatoes
6 hard-boiled eggs, sliced
1 can cream of chicken soup
1 c. milk
¹/₈ t. oregano

¹/₂ t. onion salt
¹/₈ t. pepper
¹/₄ t. garlic salt
1 T. minced onion
1 c. shredded cheddar cheese

Fry bacon until crisp; crumble. Brush a 2 qt. casserole with bacon drippings. Layer potatoes, bacon and eggs in casserole. Blend soup, milk, oregano, onion salt, pepper, garlic salt and onion; pour over potato mixture. Sprinkle cheese over top and bake at 375° for 35-40 minutes. Serves 4-6 people.

CREAMY POTATO STICKS

¹/₄ c. flour
¹/₂ t. salt
1¹/₂ c. milk
1 can cream of mushroom soup

¹/₂ lb. Velveeta cheese
1 c. chopped onions
5-6 large potatoes

In a saucepan, combine flour and salt; gradually whisk in milk until smooth. Bring to a boil; cook and stir for 2 minutes. Remove from heat; whisk in soup and cheese until smooth. Cut potatoes in sticks; place in baking dish; sprinkle with onions. Top with cheese sauce. Bake uncovered at 350° for 1 hour or until potatoes are tender. Sprinkle with paprika. Serves 6 people.

Mrs. Dan J. (Mary) Miller

Love is . . . silence—when our words would hurt; patience—when our neighbor's curt! Deafness—when the scandal flows; thoughtfulness—for others' woes!

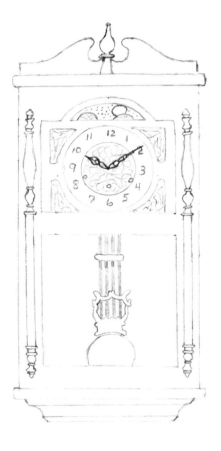

This clock is a special piece of furniture on our living room wall. This was my birthday gift from Aden when I turned 20, my last birthday before we got married. Part of the reason it's so special is because Aden spent a lot of time designing it, and I've never seen one exactly like it. On our wedding day it hung on the wall by the "eck."

MEATS & MAIN DISHES

ZESTY LEMON POTATOES

2 medium red potatoes
2 t. minced fresh parsley
2 t. olive oil
1 t. lemon juice

$^1/_2$ t. grated lemon peel
$^1/_4$ t. salt
$^1/_8$ t. pepper

Cut potatoes into $^1/_2$" cubes. Cover with water; boil until almost tender. Combine remaining ingredients. Drain potatoes; add lemon mixture and toss to coat.

SEASONED FAN POTATOES

4 medium potatoes
2 t. taco seasoning
1 t. salt
2 T. butter, melted

4 T. finely shredded cheese
2 T. grated Parmesan cheese
2 T. minced fresh parsley

With a sharp knife, slice potatoes thinly but not all the way through, leaving slices attached at the bottom. Fan potatoes slightly. Place in an ungreased baking dish. Sprinkle with taco seasoning and salt. Drizzle with butter. Bake uncovered at 425° for 50 minutes. Sprinkle with cheeses and parsley; bake 10-15 minutes longer until lightly browned.

tips and hints

WHEN MAKING PAN GRAVY ADD A BIT

OF INSTANT COFFEE GRANULES FOR

EXTRA FLAVOR AND COLOR.

Wooden Spoon Wedding Cookbook   **51**

CRUNCHY POTATO BALLS

2 c. stiff mashed potatoes
2 c. chopped fully cooked ham
$^1/_4$ c. shredded cheddar or Swiss
    cheese
$^1/_3$ c. salad dressing

1 egg, beaten
1 t. mustard
$^1/_4$ t. pepper
2-4 T. flour
$1^3/_4$ c. crushed cornflakes

In a bowl combine potatoes, ham, cheese, salad dressing, egg, mustard and
pepper; mix well. Add enough flour to make a stiff mixture. Chill. Shape
into 1" balls; roll in cornflakes. Place on a greased cookie sheet. Bake at
350° for 25-30 minutes. Serve hot. This is a good way to use up leftover
mashed potatoes. Any leftover meat, chopped up fine, is good. Yield: approximately 6 dozen.

CRISPY POTATO WEDGES

2 t. paprika
2 t. dried parsley flakes
$^1/_2$ t. onion salt

1 t. pepper
4 medium potatoes, cut into wedges
$^2/_3$ c. butter, melted

In a Zip-Lock bag combine the seasonings. Dip potatoes into melted
butter; place in bag and shake to coat. Arrange in a single layer on an
ungreased baking sheet. Bake at 450° for 25-30 minutes or until tender.

tips and hints

WHEN HARD-BOILING EGGS ADD A

LITTLE SALT TO KEEP

THEM FROM CRACKING.

MEATS & MAIN DISHES

CHEESEBURGER 'N FRIES CASSEROLE

2 lb. lean ground beef
1 (10³/₄ oz.) can cream of
   mushroom soup
1 (10³/₄ oz.) can condensed cheddar
   cheese soup

20 oz. frozen crinkle cut
   french fries

Brown hamburger; drain. Stir in soups. Pour into a greased 13" x 9" x 2"
baking dish. Arrange french fries on top. Bake, uncovered, at 350° for 50-
55 minutes or until fries are golden brown.

BEEF BURGER PIE

1 lb. ground beef
¹/₄ c. chopped onion
2 T. butter
2 T. flour
1 t. salt

2 c. tomatoes, cooked
1 c. diced carrots, cooked
1 c. diced potatoes, cooked
1 t. Worcestershire sauce
¹/₄ t. pepper

Cheese Puff Topping:
1 c. all-purpose flour
1¹/₂ t. baking powder
¹/₂ t. dry mustard
¹/₄ c. grated cheese or powdered
   cheddar cheese

2 T. shortening
1 c. milk

Brown beef with onion and butter. Add salt and pepper. Stir in flour. Then
add the rest of ingredients and cook a little. Pour into a casserole dish (2
qt. size) and top with cheese puff topping. For cheese puff topping, mix dry
ingredients. Cut in shortening. Add milk and mix. Drop on casserole by
tablespoons. Bake at 350° for 30 minutes.

Mrs. Ivan A. Miller

Love is like wildflowers—found in the most unlikely places.

Wooden Spoon Wedding Cookbook   **53**

QUICK AND EASY BREAKFAST

4 slices bread
1 lb. sausage
1 c. shredded cheese
6 eggs, beaten

2 c. milk
1 t. dry mustard
1 t. salt
dash of pepper

Put bread, torn in pieces, in baking dish. Brown sausage and put over
bread. Sprinkle cheese over sausage. Mix eggs, milk, mustard, salt and
pepper together. Pour over the rest of ingredients. Bake at 350° for 30 minutes. This is a good way to use up old bread, and we also like it for supper
instead of breakfast. Serves 5 people.

CHEESEBURGER PIE

$1/2$ lb. hamburger
$1/3$ c. onion, chopped
$1/2$ c. mayonnaise
$1/2$ c. milk
3 eggs, beaten

$1 1/2$ c. grated cheese
$1/2$ t. salt
$1/8$ t. pepper
$1/8$ t. oregano

Brown hamburger and onion; drain well. Beat together milk, mayonnaise
and seasonings. Stir in beaten eggs. Add hamburger and cheese. Pour into
baked pie shell. Bake at 350° for 35-40 minutes.

tips and hints

IN THE COURSE OF A LIFETIME A HUMAN BEING

EATS 50 TONS OF FOOD AND DRINKS 11,000

GALLONS OF LIQUID.

MAPLE FRENCH TOAST

12 slices bread, cubed
8 oz. cream cheese, cubed
8 eggs
1 c. milk
$1/2$ c. maple syrup

Arrange half of the bread cubes in a greased shallow 2 qt. baking dish. Top with cream cheese and remaining bread. In a bowl, whisk eggs, milk and syrup; pour over bread. Cover and refrigerate overnight. Remove from the refrigerator 30 minutes before baking. Cover and bake at 350° for 30 minutes. Uncover; bake 20-25 minutes longer or until golden brown. Serve with additional syrup. Serves 8 people.

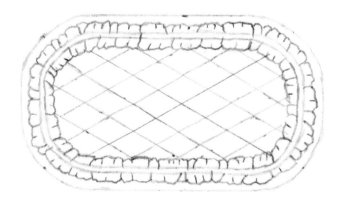

I enjoyed sewing six of these placemats which were used in the "eck." I used dark blue material with a white lace ruffle.

Our witnesses got to keep their placemats.

PIZZA CASSEROLE

2 lb. hamburger	1¹/₃ c. flour
1 medium onion	¹/₄ t. salt
2 T. butter	¹/₄ c. oil
2 c. spaghetti	2 t. baking powder
1 pt. peas	³/₄ c. milk
2 c. pizza sauce	1 c. sour cream
1 c. ketchup	3¹/₂ T. salad dressing
1 qt. potatoes	2 c. shredded cheese

Fry hamburger and onion in butter. Cook spaghetti and cubed potatoes. Make dough with flour, salt, baking powder, oil and milk. Press dough in bottom of medium sized roaster. Add meat, spaghetti, potatoes and peas in layers. Pour pizza sauce and ketchup over this. Mix and add sour cream and salad dressing. Top with cheese. Bake uncovered for 1 hour at 350°.

Mrs. Henry D. (Alma) Mast

PIZZA CASSEROLE

1 lb. pkg. noodles	1 small can mushrooms
1 can mushroom soup	1 pkg. pepperoni
3 lb. sausage	mozzarella cheese
2¹/₂ pt. pizza sauce	

Cook noodles in salt water. Add mushroom soup. Brown sausage and add pizza sauce. Put mushrooms on top of noodles in a large roaster. Then put meat mixture on top of that. Last put on pepperoni and cheese to suit your taste.

Ella L. Miller

FRENCH PIZZA

1 lb. bacon or any desired meat
shredded potatoes
5-6 eggs

milk
Velveeta cheese

Fry bacon; use part of grease to fry potatoes in. First layer: Fry shredded potatoes until soft. Turn heat on low with lid on. Second layer: Stir up eggs with a little bit of milk. Third layer: Sprinkle with bacon and Velveeta cheese.

Barbara Miller

BACON CHEESEBURGER CASSEROLE

1 lb. hamburger, browned
8 slices bacon, fried
1 t. Worcestershire sauce
2¹/₂ c. shredded potatoes, cooked

5 Velveeta slices per layer
salt and pepper
¹/₄ c. onion
1 can celery soup

Sauté onions in a little bacon grease. Add browned hamburger and crumbled bacon. Add celery soup, Worcestershire sauce and seasonings. Put a layer of potatoes in a greased 2 qt. casserole. Top with ¹/₂ of the meat and cheese slices. Repeat. Cover and bake at 400° for 45 minutes.

Mrs. David (Anna) Miller

True love is a gift on which no return is demanded. To love unselfishly is its own reward. To love for fulfillment, satisfaction or pride is not love.

BACON CHEESEBURGER RICE

1 lb. hamburger	$^1/_2$ t. pepper
1$^3/_4$ c. water	1$^1/_2$ c. rice, cooked
$^2/_3$ c. barbecue sauce	1 c. shredded cheese
1 T. mustard	$^1/_3$ c. chopped dill pickles
2 T. finely chopped onion	5 bacon strips, cooked and crumbled

In a saucepan over medium heat, cook beef until no longer pink; drain. Add water, barbecue sauce, mustard, onion and pepper. Bring to a boil; stir in the rice. Sprinkle with cheese. Reduce heat; cover and simmer for 5 minutes. Sprinkle with pickles and bacon. I like to substitute the hamburger with bulk sausage and the bacon with ham. We are not really rice eaters, but we like this recipe.

LASAGNA

16 oz. lasagna noodles, cooked	$^1/_4$ c. Parmesan cheese
2 lb. hamburger, browned	1 large carton cottage cheese
2 qt. pizza sauce	$^1/_2$ t. salt
3 eggs	1 c. sour cream
$^1/_4$ t. pepper	6 c. mozzarella cheese

Put browned hamburger and pizza sauce in pan and simmer 15 minutes. Mix cottage cheese, beaten eggs, sour cream, Parmesan cheese, salt and pepper. Layer in 2 oblong pans: Hamburger mixture, noodles, egg mixture, mozzarella cheese. Continue layers until pans are full. Bake at 350° for 45 minutes. I like to add some Velveeta cheese yet.

Mrs. Andy J. (Clara) Yoder

SAUERKRAUT CASSEROLE

1¹/₂ lb. raw sausage or sausage
   wieners
1¹/₂ c. sauerkraut

6 medium potatoes
4 oz. sour cream
layer of shredded cheese

Put sauerkraut in bottom of a 3 qt. casserole dish. Add sausage or sausage
wieners. Bake at 350° for 1 hour, covered. Make mashed potatoes and put
on top of sauerkraut and meat. Top with sour cream. Bake 30 minutes
longer. Add cheese 5 minutes before it's done.

Mrs. Jacob (Esther) Miller

CHICKEN POT PIE

Crust:

2 c. flour
¹/₂ c. milk
2 T. lard

1¹/₂ t. baking powder
salt to taste

Filling:

1 qt. chicken broth
1 c. potatoes, cooked
1¹/₂ c. carrots, cooked

1 c. chicken, cooked
1 c. celery, cooked

Melt 1 T. butter and mix with 3 T. flour until creamy. Use to thicken
chicken broth. Add vegetables and chicken. Put in cake pan. Top with
crust. Bake at 350°.

Alma Miller

People don't need our advice as much as our love.

CHICKEN AND BISCUITS

Dough:

2 c. flour

$^1/_2$ c. milk

$1^1/_2$ t. baking powder

2 T. butter

salt to taste

Slice desired amount of potatoes about ¼" thick. Cook until almost tender and put in baking dish. Add 1 qt. cooked chicken. Take chicken broth and make gravy. Add seasonings as desired. Pour over potatoes and chicken and top with biscuits. Bake at 375°-400° until biscuits are done.

Mrs. Jacob (Esther) Miller

CHICKEN AND BISCUITS

1 (16 oz.) pkg. frozen mixed
  vegetables

$2^1/_2$ c. cubed chicken, cooked

1 ($10^3/_4$ oz.) can cream of chicken soup

$^3/_4$ c. milk

$1^1/_2$ c. shredded cheddar
  cheese, divided

Biscuits:

1½ c. biscuit/baking mix

⅔ c. milk

In a large bowl, combine the vegetables, chicken, soup, milk and 1 c. cheese. Pour into an ungreased 13" x 9" x 2" baking dish. Cover and bake at 400° for 15 minutes. Meanwhile, in another bowl, combine biscuit mix and milk. Drop batter by tablespoons onto chicken mixture. Bake uncovered for 20-22 minutes or until biscuits are golden brown. Top with remaining cheese. Bake 3-4 minutes longer or until cheese is melted. Serves 6 people.

Mrs. Ervin (Mary) Byler

CHICKEN CASSEROLE

12 slices toasted bread crumbs
4 c. chopped chicken, cooked
1 small can cream of mushroom
   soup
1 c. chicken broth

$^1/_2$ c. salad dressing
4 eggs, beaten well
2 c. milk
1 t. salt

Bake in a 350° oven for 1 hour or until done. Can be topped with Velveeta cheese or a chicken gravy. Serves 8 or more people.

Mrs. Mahlon (Katie) Miller

CHICKEN GUMBO

9 slices bread
4 c. cut-up chicken
$^1/_4$ c. melted butter
$^1/_2$ c. salad dressing
4 eggs, beaten
1 c. milk

1 c. chicken broth
salt to taste
9 slices Velveeta cheese
2 cans cream of celery soup
buttered bread crumbs

Butter bottom of medium roaster; put 9 slices bread in bottom layer. Add cut-up chicken. Mix butter, salad dressing, beaten eggs, milk, broth and salt; pour over bread and chicken. Top with Velveeta cheese and celery soup and cover with bread crumbs. Bake in 350° oven for $1^1/_4$ hours. Cover with foil. Take foil off last 15 minutes to crisp bread. May be made and refrigerated the day before.

Barbara Miller

MACARONI HAM CASSEROLE

2 t. salt
4 oz. elbow macaroni
3 c. boiling water
1 T. oleo
$^1/_4$ c. chopped green pepper
$^1/_4$ c. chopped onion

1 c. diced ham
1 can cream of mushroom soup
$^1/_2$ c. milk
1 T. parsley
$^1/_8$ t. pepper
$^1/_2$ c. grated American cheese

Add salt and macaroni to boiling water. Boil rapidly, stirring constantly, for 2 minutes. Cover, remove from heat and let stand 10 minutes. Melt oleo in saucepan. Add green pepper and onion. Simmer 5 minutes. Add diced ham and brown lightly. Rinse macaroni with warm water and drain. Combine ham mixture, mushroom soup, milk, parsley and pepper with macaroni. Put in $1^1/_2$ qt. greased casserole dish; sprinkle with cheese and bake at 375° for 45 minutes.

EASY WIGGLERS

3 c. uncooked spaghetti
1 pt. crumbled hamburger
$^1/_2$ pt. peas
1 pt. dressing mix
  (carrots and potatoes)

1 can mushroom soup
2 c. catsup
1 t. salt
1 onion, chopped

Cook spaghetti until soft; add the rest of ingredients. Heat till hot then top with cheese. Can be made in oven or on top of stove. Makes about 4 qt.

Mrs. Dan J. (Mary) Miller

DRESSING (OR STUFFING)

5 eggs
2 c. milk
4 c. toasted bread, cut in chunks
$^1/_2$ c. cubed potatoes, cooked
$^1/_2$ c. diced carrots, cooked
$^1/_2$ c. finely diced celery

$^1/_2$ c. diced, cooked chicken with
   broth
$^1/_2$ small onion, finely chopped
2 t. salt
1 t. chicken soup base
$^1/_4$ t. pepper

Beat eggs; add milk and bread. Let stand till bread is soaked through. Add vegetables, chicken, onion and seasonings. Grease a 9" x 13" loaf pan with butter. Pour mixture in pan and bake at 375° till set and browned on top. If using canned dressing mix, use 1 qt. This is a family size recipe for the wedding dressing recipe.

HAM AND GREEN BEAN CASSEROLE

$^1/_2$ c. margarine
3 c. milk
$^1/_2$ c. flour
$1^1/_2$ c. grated Velveeta cheese

6 medium potatoes, cooked
   and diced
1 qt. green beans
3 c. diced ham

Melt margarine; stir in flour and add milk. Stir over low heat until thickened. Add cheese and allow to melt. Mix potatoes, green beans, ham and sauce in casserole. Bake at 350° for 30 minutes.

Miriam Miller

Love is giving people the freedom to be the way they are, not trying to make them the way you want them to be.

3 LB. NOODLES

1 c. butter, browned
2 qt. broth
5^{1}/$_{2}$ qt. water

^{1}/$_{4}$ jar chicken base
2 t. salt
3 lb. noodles

Bring first five ingredients to a boil—add noodles. Boil again. Remove from heat and let set 1 hour. Make some chicken gravy and add ^{1}/$_{2}$ box Velveeta cheese. When melted add to noodles.

Mrs. John D. (Katie) Miller

PIZZA

4 c. flour
6 t. baking powder
^{2}/$_{3}$ c. Wesson oil

2 t. salt
1^{1}/$_{3}$ c. milk

Combine dry ingredients; add milk and oil. Press into a large cookie sheet. Top with pizza sauce, sausage, bologna, peppers, onions, pepperoni or whatever you wish. Bake at 350° for 1 hour. Top with cheese once it's baked. Put in oven to melt. A quick and delicious supper.

Mrs. Leroy (Katie) Miller

TACO SHELLS

1^{1}/$_{2}$ c. cold water
1 c. all-purpose flour
^{1}/$_{2}$ c. cornmeal

^{1}/$_{4}$ t. salt
1 egg

Mix all ingredients together with hand beater and fry like pancakes. Pour scant ^{1}/$_{4}$ c. dough in pan and rotate pan to make a nice round ring. Delicious when served with browned hamburger, peppers, tomatoes, heated kidney beans, lettuce, shredded cheese and onions. Pour mild taco sauce and sweet-n-sour dressing over all and top with sour cream.

Mrs. Jacob D. (Esther) Miller

TORTILLA ROLL-UPS

flour tortilla shells
sour cream
lettuce, chopped
sloppy joe

tomatoes, chopped
shredded cheddar cheese
Dorito chips, crushed

Heat tortilla shells as instructed on package. Spread sour cream on tortilla shells, then add a little of rest of ingredients. Roll up and enjoy!

Mrs. John (Fannie) Miller

DUMPLINGS

2 c. flour
1 t. salt
4 t. baking powder

2 eggs, beaten
$^1/_2$ c. milk

Sift flour, baking powder and salt. Place eggs in 1 cup measure; add $^1/_2$ c. milk or more to make 1 cup. Add to flour mixture and stir till smooth and stiff, but do not overbeat. Drop by spoonsful on hot steaming chicken or stew or any potatoes or hot dish. Steam over low heat for 10-15 minutes. Do not lift cover.

Verba Miller

An act of love, no matter how great or small, is always appreciated.

tips and hints

USE YOUR FAVORITE BISCUIT RECIPE. SPOON WARM
THICKENED GRAPES OVER BISCUITS AND ADD MILK
FOR A QUICK DELICIOUS SUPPER.

DANDELION GRAVY

5 slices bacon, crumbled
2 T. flour
1 c. milk
¹/₄ t. salt

1 T. salad dressing
1 T. brown sugar
3 hard-boiled eggs, chopped
dandelion leaves

Fry five slices of bacon. Take bacon out of pan and add flour to the bacon grease. Stir; add milk. Stir, and add rest of ingredients. Last add enough dandelion leaves to suit your taste. This is a recipe that comes from Aden's family. I was very skeptical when he wanted me to make it. But with the taste of bacon and hard-boiled eggs, it's not only edible, but also very good!

FRIED SQUASH BLOSSOMS

¹/₂ c. flour
¹/₂ t. baking powder
¹/₄ t. garlic salt
¹/₄ t. ground cumin
1 egg

¹/₂ c. milk
1 T. vegetable oil
12 large freshly picked
  squash blossoms

Combine flour, baking powder, garlic salt and cumin. In another bowl, beat egg, milk and oil; add to dry ingredients and stir until smooth. Dip blossoms into batter and fry in oil until crisp. Drain on paper towels. Keep warm until serving. Note: Pumpkin blossoms are also good.

MEATS & MAIN DISHES

BAKED ONION RINGS

1½ c. crushed cornflakes
2 t. sugar
1 t. paprika
¼ t. seasoned salt

¼ t. garlic salt
2 large sweet onions
2 eggs

Combine first five ingredients; set aside. Cut onions into ½" thick slices. Separate into rings, reserving the small rings for another use. Beat eggs. Dip onion rings into eggs, then into crumb mixture, coating well. Place in a single layer on greased baking sheets. Bake at 375° for 15-20 minutes or until onions are tender and coating is crisp. Serves 6 people.

FRIED DILL PICKLE COINS

2 c. flour
½ t. salt
¼ t. pepper

2 eggs
1 c. milk
3 c. dill pickles

Mix first three ingredients. In another bowl beat eggs and milk. Blot pickles dry with paper towels. Coat with flour mixture; dip into egg mixture and coat again with flour. Deep-fat fry for about 10 minutes. Serve warm with Ranch dressing.

Wooden Spoon Wedding Cookbook **67**

NOTES

Soups & Vegetables

Many choose mixed vegetables for their wedding day,
And if that's what they like, they really may.
But to me frozen corn is the way to go,
Even if not everyone may think so.

The butter had to be nice and brown;
Now please turn the burner way down.
Next the corn into the saucepan you pour,
Twelve pounds and no more.

Thirty-six pounds of corn was made that eve;
Just a bit was left when the people started to leave.
The rest was heated for lunch the next day,
For the helpers who decided to stay.

And now my son inherited from me,
For he loves sweet corn, you see.
For the little guy he is, he'll eat a pile,
Talking and smiling all the while.

Mixed Vegetables

2 lb. mixed vegetables
$^1/_2$ c. butter
1 can cream of mushroom soup
$^1/_2$ c. milk
$^1/_2$ c. Velveeta cheese

Cook vegetables until tender. While vegetables cook, brown butter.
Add mushroom soup and milk. Make a smooth sauce, adding cheese
last. Drain vegetables and add sauce. Add salt to taste. We had 40 lb.
vegetables for our wedding for supper.

Andy & Lizzie Miller

CHEESEBURGER SOUP

10 lb. hamburger, browned
$4^1/_2$ c. onions
$4^1/_2$ c. carrots
$4^1/_2$ c. celery
$4^1/_2$ t. salt
1 T. pepper
1 T. sweet basil
2 T. parsley
18 c. chicken broth
24 c. potatoes
$2^1/_2$ T. chicken base

Dice or chop all vegetables. Mix all together and cold pack for 3 hours.
When opening, brown a little butter and 2 T. flour for 1 qt. soup. Add some
milk to suit taste and Velveeta cheese.

Mrs. Uriah (Sevilla) Yoder

CHEESEBURGER SOUP

1 lb. hamburger, browned
   and drained
$^1/_2$ c. grated carrots
$^1/_3$ c. chopped celery
2 (11 oz.) cans cheddar cheese
   soup or Velveeta cheese

salt and pepper to taste
2 c. cooked rice
$^1/_4$ c. chopped onions
3 c. chicken broth
2 soup cans milk
1 (8 oz.) container sour cream

Combine broth, carrots, onions and celery. Simmer for 10 minutes. Add meat, rice, cheese and milk. Add sour cream last. Do not boil. Yield: 3 qt.

Supper time comes. Oh, what shall it be? "Well, children, what are you hungry for?"

"Oklahoma Soup—Oklahoma Soup!" which is this cheeseburger soup. We had been in a family get-together in Oklahoma, and this soup was served for supper.

Mrs. David (Anna) Miller

CHEESEBURGER SOUP

1 lb. hamburger, browned
$^1/_3$ c. onions
1 pt. chicken broth
$^3/_4$ c. shredded carrots
$^3/_4$ c. shredded celery

1 c. shredded potatoes
$^3/_4$ t. salt
$^1/_3$ t. pepper
1 cube or $2^1/_4$ t. chicken seasoning

Fry onions with hamburger. Add rest of ingredients and bring to a boil until vegetables are tender but not too soft. Add 1 pt. water if vegetables are too thick. To make white sauce melt $^1/_4$ c. butter; add $^1/_2$ c. flour (scant). Let brown a little. Add $1^1/_2$ to 2 c. milk and stir until boiling (it will be thick). Slowly add $^1/_3$ box Velveeta cheese. Stir until melted. Add white sauce to boiling vegetables and hamburger mixture. Very good. Yield: 3 qt.

Ella L. Miller

Everyone who has a part at a wedding receives a gift for their help. In February we started some violet plants. Aden's mom also did some for us. We had close to 40 violet plants to take care of. The evening before the wedding we arranged them on the windowsills in the shop. So they decorated the shop for the wedding and every tablewaiter chose one to take along home. They also received a Wooden Spoon Cookbook, signed by the author.

POTATO SOUP

1 qt. diced potatoes
2 lb. hamburger
2 T. butter

4 T. flour
water

Cook potatoes in a large saucepan; fry hamburger in butter. Sprinkle flour over meat and mix. Add water to make a gravy. Bring to a boil and add to potatoes. Serve over crackers. Canned hamburger works fine.

Years ago my maternal grandparents had unexpected company one day. Grandma asked them to stay for dinner. Not wanting her to go to a lot of work, they said they'd stay if she would make soup. And this is the soup she made, as her original recipe said, "Good enough for company."

CHUNKY CHICKEN SOUP (TO CAN)

2 gal. water
6 qt. chicken broth
$^{1}/_{2}$ c. chicken base
$^{1}/_{4}$ c. butter
$^{1}/_{2}$ c. salt
2 qt. celery
2 qt. carrots

3 qt. peas
4 qt. potatoes
8 lb. cut-up chicken, cooked
2 onions
handful parsley
$4^{1}/_{2}$ c. flour or Perma-Flo

Cook vegetables. Drain; use this water for some of the water in the soup. Heat water, broth, base, butter and salt to boiling. Make a paste with flour and add to boiling mixture. Add chicken and vegetables. Pressure can at 10 lbs. for 40 minutes or cold pack for 3 hours. Yield: Approx. 17 qt.

Rebecca Yoder

Wooden Spoon Wedding Cookbook 73

SOUPS & VEGETABLES

ONION CHEESE SOUP

1 large onion, chopped	pepper to taste
3 T. butter	4 c. milk
3 T. flour	2 c. shredded cheese
$^1/_2$ t. salt	

In a large saucepan sauté onions in butter. Stir in flour, salt and pepper until blended. Gradually add milk. Bring to a boil; cook and stir for 2 minutes or until thickened. Stir in cheese until melted. Serve with crackers or seasoned salad croutons. Serves 6 people.

CHILI SOUP

$1^1/_2$ lb. ground beef	$^1/_2$ t. cinnamon
1 c. chopped onion	$^1/_2$ t. paprika
1 qt. pizza sauce	1 t. garlic powder
3 c. water	2 T. brown sugar
1 (15.5 oz.) can kidney beans	$^1/_2$ t. salt
4 T. chili powder	

Cook ground beef and onion in large saucepan until no longer pink. Add rest of ingredients. Bring to a boil. Cook 10-15 minutes. Serve.

Mrs. Ervin (Mary) Byler

tips and hints

ON AVERAGE THERE ARE EIGHT

PEAS IN A POD.

CABBAGE CHOWDER

4 c. coarsely shredded cabbage
3 c. diced potatoes
2 c. diced carrots
1 T. salt
1 t. sugar

$^1/_4$ t. pepper
3 c. water
4 c. scalded milk
2 T. butter

Cook all ingredients except milk and butter for 10 minutes or until tender.
Add milk and butter. Eat like soup. We use saltines and often add a little
more pepper. Delicious on a cold winter evening!

Mrs. David D. (Emma) Miller

CHEESY CHICKEN CHOWDER

4 c. chunked potatoes
4 c. sliced carrots
1 medium onion, finely sliced
chicken broth and chicken pieces
4 c. milk

chicken soup base to taste
Velveeta to taste
salt to taste
4 heaping T. flour

Put potatoes, carrots and onions in saucepan. Add broth to cover well.
Cook until soft, then add half of milk, chicken pieces, salt and soup
base. Bring to a boil and add a white sauce of flour and rest of milk. Add
Velveeta last. Serve with crackers. A quick shortcut for this soup is to use
canned dressing vegetables (carrots and potatoes) and canned chicken.
Add other ingredients to suit your family's taste.

Mrs. John (Katie) Troyer

tips and hints

BEFORE HEATING PIZZA, DAMPEN THE OUTSIDE CRUST
WITH WATER TO KEEP IT FROM GETTING SO HARD.

A friend is one to whom one may pour out the contents of one's heart, chaff and grain together, knowing that the gentlest of hands will take and sift it, keep what is worth keeping and with a breath of kindness blow the rest away.

ESCALLOPED CORN

1 pt. corn
1 t. salt
dash of pepper
3 T. butter, melted

1 t. sugar
³/₄ c. crushed cracker crumbs
2 eggs, beaten well
1¹/₄ c. milk

Mix all together and put in 1¹/₂ qt. buttered casserole dish. Bake at 350° for one hour. This is a good way to make the last of your fresh corn go furthur.

CARROT CASSEROLE

5 c. sliced carrots
2 large onions, diced

¹/₃ c. butter
¹/₂ lb. Velveeta cheese, sliced

Cook carrots until almost tender. Sauté onions in butter. Layer carrots in a 2 qt. casserole dish alternately with sliced Velveeta. Pour onions and butter over carrots. Bake at 350° for 30 minutes.

CHEDDAR HAM SOUP

2 c. peeled, diced potatoes
2 c. water
½ c. sliced carrots
¼ c. chopped onion
¼ c. butter, cubed
flour

2 c. milk
¼-½ t. salt
¼ t. pepper
2 c. shredded cheddar cheese
1½ c. cubed ham, fully cooked
1 c. frozen peas, thawed

Combine potatoes, carrots, onions and water. Bring to a boil. Reduce heat; cover and cook for 10-15 minutes or until tender. In another saucepan melt butter. Stir in flour until smooth. Gradually add milk, salt and pepper. Bring to a boil; cook and stir for 2 minutes or until thickened. Stir in cheese until melted. Stir into undrained potato mixture. Add ham and peas; heat through. Serves 7 people.

You can give without loving, but you can't love without giving.

tips and hints

WHEN PIZZA NEEDS TO BE HEATED, SAVE YOURSELF
FROM WASHING A DIRTY PAN AND LEAVE THE PIZZA
ON THE CARDBOARD.

NOTES

Pies

When the time came to decide on pie,
Apple, surprise pecan and peanut butter were tie.
And so it was settled, we'll have all three,
Each on his own can decide what it will be.

The wedding day is drawing nigh,
And so it's time to bake the pie.
On Tuesday they cooked the filling;
It didn't take long; many hands were willing!

Grandpa peeled the apples; aunts baked the pie,
And by noon they finished with a sigh.
Twenty apple, fifteen surprise pecan and fifteen peanut butter;
To look at them almost makes my heart flutter.

Usually pies don't really touch my heart,
But these pies in our wedding would be a part.
I could hardly grasp it, a wedding for Aden and I.
Could I be a good wife? Oh, how hard I'll try!

Aden and Miriam
October 2, 2003

Apple Pie

12 c. sliced apples
3 c. white sugar

6 T. tapioca
3 c. water

Crumbs:
10 c. rolled oats
3 1/3 c. brown sugar
3 c. nuts

5 t. cinnamon
3 c. butter

Put apples through Salad Master. Mix apples, sugar, water and tapioca. Put in unbaked pie shells. Mix topping ingredients and put on top of apples. Bake at 425°. Filling is enough for 5 pies and crumbs is enough for 10 pies.

We rented four gas ovens to be used at the wedding. They were delivered a few days before the wedding, so we had four ovens to bake these 20 apple pies. My 89-year-old maternal grandparents put the apples through the apple peeler and my paternal grandma cut the apples. Two of my aunts baked the pies the day before the wedding. We made two batches of crumbs on Tuesday already.

Aden and Miriam
October 2, 2003

Peanut Butter Pie

10 c. milk
2½ c. white sugar
1⅔ c. flour

3 eggs
10 egg yolks

Crumbs:
11¼ c. powdered sugar
5 c. peanut butter

2 t. salt

Heat milk. Mix the rest of ingredients and add to milk. Bring to a boil. Remove from heat. Add ¼ c. butter and 5 t. vanilla. Put ½ c. crumbs in bottom of baked pie shell. Fill with filling; top with whipped topping. Sprinkle some crumbs on top.

This is Dad's favorite pie, so that's what made me choose it for our wedding. On Friday before the wedding we baked 15 pie shells and made 1 batch of the crumbs. Then on Tuesday we cooked 3 batches of the filling. It didn't take quite all the crumbs to make the 15 pies, but we didn't have many pies left over.

Aden and Miriam
October 2, 2003

Surprise Pecan Pie

2 c. brown sugar
2 c. white sugar
1 c. margarine
12 eggs, beaten
3 c. light corn syrup

1 t. salt
4 t. vanilla
2 c. chocolate chips
2 c. pecans

Cream margarine and sugars. Add next four ingredients. In each pie shell put $1/2$ c. chocolate chips and $1/2$ c. pecans. Pour filling over it. Bake at 375° for 40-45 minutes. Allow time to set before serving. Yield: 4 pies.

Fifteen of these pies were baked the day before the wedding. Though not a very popular pie, it must have been a hit as we didn't have many left over. We got this recipe from a friend and experimented with it until we were satisfied. It is a family favorite!

Imitation Pecan Pie

$^1/_2$ c. grape nuts
$^1/_2$ c. lukewarm water
$^1/_2$ c. white sugar
$^1/_4$ t. salt
$^1/_2$ t. vanilla
2 eggs, beaten

1 c. green label Karo or any
   pancake syrup
$^1/_2$ t. walnut or maple flavoring
1 T. butter, melted
$^1/_4$ c. nuts

Soak grape nuts in lukewarm water. Meanwhile mix rest of ingredients together. Mix grape nuts and water into rest of ingredients and pour into an unbaked 9" pie shell and bake at 375°. This was served at our wedding in 1967.

Mrs. Jacob (Esther) Miller

APPLE PIE

2 c. raw apples
1 c. sugar

$^1/_2$ c. water
2 T. tapioca

Crumbs:
1 c. rolled oats
$^1/_3$ c. brown sugar
$^1/_3$ c. nuts

$^1/_3$ c. butter
$^1/_2$ t. cinnamon

Put apples through Salad Master. Mix apples, sugar, water and tapioca. Put in unbaked pie shell. Mix topping ingredients and put on top of apples. Bake at 425°. Yield: 1 pie.

MAGIC APPLE PIE

1 egg
3/4 c. sugar
1/2 c. flour
1 t. baking powder

pinch of salt
1 medium tart apple, peeled
and diced
1/2 c. raisins

Beat egg; add sugar, flour, baking powder and salt. Stir in apples and raisins. Spread into a greased pie plate. Bake at 350° for 25-30 minutes or until golden brown and a toothpick inserted near the center comes out clean. Serve with whipped topping or ice cream if desired.

FRESH PEAR PIE

3/4 c. white sugar
3 T. quick-cooking tapioca
2 T. lemon juice
2 T. butter, cubed
1 t. grated lemon peel

1/2 t. nutmeg
1/2 t. cinnamon
1/4 t. salt
6 lb. ripe pears, peeled and sliced

Combine first eight ingredients. Add pears; toss to coat. Pour into an unbaked pie crust. For a fancy look, cut dough into eight 1/2" strips. Twist strips and position over filling parallel to each other, approximately 1/2" apart. Trim strips even with pastry edge. Brush strips with milk. Cover pie loosely with foil to prevent over-browning. Bake at 400° for 50-60 minutes or until crust is golden brown and filling is bubbly.

tips and hints

BEFORE BAKING PIES, BRUSH THE TOP WITH MILK
AND SPRINKLE WITH SUGAR. LEAVES A NICE,
BROWN, CRUSTY TOP.

MRS. DAN (EMMA) MILLER

LEMON MERINGUE PIE

1½ c. sugar
⅓ c. plus 1 T. cornstarch
1½ c. water
3 egg yolks

3 T. butter
lemon peel
½ c. lemon juice

Meringue:
3 egg whites
¼ t. cream of tartar

6 T. sugar
½ t. vanilla

Mix sugar and cornstarch. Gradually stir in water. Cook over medium
heat, stirring constantly, until mixture thickens and boils. Boil one minute.
Gradually stir half of the hot mixture into egg yolks. Blend into hot mixture. Boil and stir one minute. Remove from heat; stir in butter, lemon peel
and juice. Pour into baked pie shell. For meringue: Beat egg whites and
cream of tartar until foamy. Beat in sugar, 1 T. at a time. Continue beating
until stiff and glossy. Do not underbeat. Add vanilla. Heap meringue onto
hot pie filling. Spread over filling, sealing meringue to edge of crust. Bake
approximately 10 minutes or until a delicate brown.

Erma Miller

tips and hints

BRUSH THE INSIDE OF THE BOTTOM PIE CRUST

WITH BEATEN EGG WHITES BEFORE BAKING.

PREVENTS SOGGING.

MRS. DAN (EMMA) MILLER

RASPBERRY PIE

2 t. gelatin	3 c. milk, divided
2 T. cold water	2 T. butter
sugar	2 T. vanilla
cornstarch	1 c. whipped topping
egg yolks	

Top Part:

1 qt. raspberry juice (or any fruit)	7 heaping T. clear jel
1 qt. water	2 c. water
2 c. sugar	raspberry Jell-O, optional
1 t. salt	

Soak gelatin in cold water. Mix sugar, cornstarch, egg yolks and 1 c. milk. Heat 2 c. milk; add mixture of sugar, etc. Bring to a boil. Remove from heat; add gelatin, butter and vanilla. When cold add whipped topping. Bring raspberry juice, 1 qt. water, sugar and salt to a boil. Mix clear jel and 2 c. water. Add to hot juice. Fill 6 baked pie shells a little over half full with eggnog filling. Top with top part.

Mrs. John D. (Katie) Miller

FRESH RASPBERRY PIE

36 large marshmallows	4 c. fresh raspberries
2 c. whipped topping	

In a double boiler heat marshmallows just until melted. Cool to room temperature. Fold in topping and raspberries. Pour mixture in a 9" baked pie shell or graham cracker crust. Chill until set.

Emma Miller

RHUBARB CREAM PIE

2 T. flour
1 c. white sugar
2 egg yolks

$^1/_2$ c. sweet milk
2 c. rhubarb, cut up fine

Mix all ingredients together and pour into an unbaked pie shell. Bake at 425° until rhubarb is tender and filling is set. Beat egg whites and add 3 T. brown sugar. Put on pie and bake until brown. Yield: 1 pie.

Mrs. Andy (Lizzie) Miller

PEANUT BUTTER PIE

$^1/_2$ c. sugar
2 T. flour
2 T. cornstarch
$^1/_2$ t. salt
$^1/_2$ c. milk
2 egg yolks

$1^1/_2$ c. milk
1 T. butter
1 t. vanilla
$^1/_3$ c. peanut butter
$^3/_4$ c. powdered sugar

Mix sugar, flour, cornstarch and salt. Set aside. Mix ½ c. milk and egg yolks. Add to flour mixture. Heat 1½ c. milk to boiling; add flour mixture. Stir until thickened. Remove from heat; add butter and vanilla. Cool. Mix peanut butter and powdered sugar. Sprinkle in bottom of baked pie shell. Reserve some for top. Pour cooked mixture on top of crumbs; top with meringue or whipped topping, and add remaining crumbs. Yield: 1 pie.

Elmina Miller

A menu like this was hung at the end of every table, so the tablewaiters knew what to serve for dinner and supper. I hand-stamped one and made copies to save some work.

PEANUT BUTTER PIE

Crust:

1¼ c. Oreo cookie crumbs
(approximately 20 cookies)

¼ c. white sugar
¼ c. butter or margarine, melted

Filling:

8 oz. cream cheese
1 c. creamy peanut butter
1 c. sugar

1 T. butter or margarine, softened
1 t. vanilla
1 c. heavy cream, whipped

Combine crust ingredients; press into a 9" pie plate. Bake at 375° for 10 minutes. Cool. In mixing bowl, beat cream cheese, peanut butter, sugar, butter and vanilla until smooth. Fold in whipped cream. Gently spoon into crust. Garnish with chocolate or cookie crumbs if desired. Refrigerate. If you are looking for a rich peanut butter dessert, you have found it. It is good with ice cream.

CHOCOLATE MOCHA PIE

1 T. gelatin
¼ c. cold water
1 T. cocoa
1 t. coffee
⅛ t. salt

¾ c. sugar
1¼ c. milk
1 c. whipped topping
1 t. vanilla

Dissolve gelatin in water. Combine the next 5 ingredients. Bring to a boil, stirring constantly. Remove from heat; add gelatin. Cool until slightly thickened; beat until smooth. Beat topping; add vanilla. Fold whipped topping into cooked mixture. Yield: 1 pie.

CHOCOLATE PIE

³/₄ c. white sugar
3 T. cocoa
¹/₄ t. salt
1¹/₂ T. butter
4 c. milk

¹/₂ c. white sugar
¹/₂ c. cornstarch (scant)
1¹/₂ T. flour
³/₄ c. milk

Mix first three ingredients in 3 qt. saucepan. Add a little water and boil until syrupy. Add butter and milk to mixture in saucepan. Bring to a boil. Mix remaining ingredients together in mixing bowl. Add slowly to mixture in saucepan and stir until boiling. Spread a little cream cheese in baked pie shell. Fill with filling. Top with whipped cream. Yield: 2 pies.

Mrs. Alvin (Ida) Miller

PECAN PIE

3 eggs, slightly beaten
1 c. light corn syrup
1 c. brown sugar (scant)
¹/₄ c. melted butter

¹/₂ t. salt
1 t. vanilla
1 c. pecan halves

Mix all together except pecans. Pour into 9" pie pan. Put pecans on top. Bake at 350° for 45-50 minutes or until center is set. Toothpick comes out clean when done.

Mrs. David D. (Emma) Miller

PECAN PIE

3 eggs, beaten
$^3/_4$ c. light Karo
1 t. vanilla
$^1/_4$ c. pancake syrup

3 T. butter, melted
$^1/_8$ t. salt
$^1/_4$ c. brown sugar
1 c. pecan pieces

Sprinkle pecans on bottom of unbaked pie shell. Mix rest of ingredients together and pour over pecans. Bake at 400° for 15 minutes. Reduce heat to 350° and bake until set.

Rebecca Yoder

RICE KRISPIE PIE

6 eggs
$^1/_2$ c. brown sugar
$1^1/_2$ c. light corn syrup
$1^1/_2$ t. flour
$^1/_2$ c. water

$^1/_2$ t. salt
1 t. vanilla
2 T. butter, melted
2 c. Rice Krispies

Beat eggs and mix in order given. Bake at 350°. Yield: 2 pies.

Mrs. John D. (Katie) Miller

Marriage is an institution held together by three books—Good, cook and check.

Wooden Spoon Wedding Cookbook   **91**

VANILLA CRUMB PIE

2 c. molasses (King syrup)
2 c. sugar
4 c. water

$^1/_2$ c. flour
2 eggs, beaten
2 t. vanilla

Crumbs:
2 c. sugar
1 c. butter
2 t. soda

1 t. cream of tartar
4 c. flour

Mix first six ingredients together. Bring to a boil and cool. Mix crumbs together. Pour syrup into an unbaked pie shell; put crumbs on top and bake at 350°. Yield: 3 large or 4 small pies.

Mrs. Ervin (Mary) Byler

MOUNDS PIE

3 eggs
1 c. light corn syrup
2 T. butter
$^1/_4$ t. salt

1 t. vanilla
$^1/_2$ c. macaroon coconut
$^1/_2$ c. oatmeal
$^1/_2$ c. chocolate chips

Beat eggs; add corn syrup, butter, vanilla and salt. Mix well. Add the remaining ingredients. Pour into an unbaked pie crust. Bake at 350° for 45 minutes or until it is set. Yield: 1 pie.

Verba Miller

Since I enjoy hand-stamping cards, I decided to make my own charts for the wedding. I made one for the cooks, one for the tablewaiters and one that said, "Supper". The cooks and tablewaiters had to find their name on the chart to see what they have to fix for dinner. Then in the afternoon they had to see the "Supper" charts to see what their job is for supper.

OATMEAL PIE

3 eggs, slightly beaten
³/₄ c. sugar
³/₄ c. light Karo
¹/₂ c. oatmeal
¹/₂ c. coconut

¹/₂ c. water
¹/₂ t. salt
1 T. butter, melted
1 t. vanilla

Mix all together, adding oatmeal and coconut last. Put in unbaked pie shell. Bake about 45 minutes. Yield: 1 pie.

Naomi E. Coblentz

COCONUT OATMEAL PIE

¹/₄ c. butter, browned a bit
¹/₂ c. sugar
¹/₂ t. cinnamon, optional
¹/₄ t. salt
³/₄ c. dark Karo, or any pancake syrup

3 eggs, well beaten
³/₄ c. water
¹/₂ c. quick oats
¹/₂ c. coconut

Melt butter, then add rest of ingredients, adding oats and coconut last. Pour into an unbaked pie crust. Bake at 425° until top is nice and brown, then lower to 350° to finish. Yield: 1 pie.

Mrs. John (Katie) Troyer

---

tips and hints

HAPPINESS IS THE FOUNDATION OF "LOVE" FROM WHICH FLOW STREAMS OF CONTENTMENT.

BLUEBERRY CUSTARD PIE

2 egg yolks
1 T. flour
salt
beaten egg whites

$^3/_4$ c. brown sugar
1$^1/_2$ c. milk
vanilla
fresh blueberries

Mix egg yolks, sugar and flour together, then add milk, salt, vanilla and beaten egg whites. Put enough fresh blueberries in unbaked pie shell to cover bottom; pour custard filling on top. Bake at 425° for 15 minutes, then at 350° until done. This is also good with black raspberries. Do not wash fruits or pies will get watery. Yield: 1 pie.

Mrs. John (Fannie) Miller

CUSTARD PIE

2 c. sugar
3 T. flour
$^1/_2$ c. butter
3 eggs, separated

3 c. milk
1 t. vanilla or maple flavoring
pinch of salt

Cream butter; add egg yolks, sugar and flour; blend well. Add milk, then fold in stiffly beaten egg whites. Pour into two pastry shells and bake at 350° until set.

Barbara Miller

If a man has enough horse sense to treat his wife like a thoroughbred she will never turn into an old nag.

Wooden Spoon Wedding Cookbook **95**

PIES

CUSTARD PIE

2 eggs, separated
2 T. butter, browned
dash of salt
$^3/_4$ c. brown sugar

1 T. flour
1 pt. milk, can be mixed
   with cream or evaporated milk

Mix egg yolks and sugar. Then add brown butter and stir real well. Add flour and salt. Then add hot milk. Last add beaten egg whites. Bake at 450° until browned, then reduce to 350° until done.

Ella L. Miller

MOTHER'S SPECIAL PUMPKIN PIE

2 c. milk
2 eggs, separated
2 T. flour
$^1/_2$ c. brown sugar

$^1/_2$ c. white sugar
$^3/_4$ c. pumpkin
$^1/_2$ t. pumpkin pie spice
$^1/_8$ t. salt

Heat milk. Beat egg yolks and add flour, sugars, pumpkin, salt and spice. Add this mixture to milk. Last of all, fold in beaten egg whites. Mix and pour into an unbaked pie crust.

My mother was known for her delicious pumpkin pies. When my dad's side got together and there were pumpkin pies served, the usual question was, "Did Reuben Mattie make these?" And if the answer was yes, there usually were none left over.

Mrs. David (Anna) Miller

96   *Wooden Spoon Wedding Cookbook*

CREAMY PUMPKIN PIE

½ c. cold milk
1 pkg. vanilla instant pudding
1 t. pumpkin pie spice

1 c. canned pumpkin
2½ c. frozen whipped topping, thawed

In a large bowl beat milk, instant pudding and spice with wire whisk for 1 minute. (Mixture will be very thick.) Whisk in pumpkin. Stir in whipped topping. Spread in crust. Enough for 1 pie. Refrigerate at least 2 hours or until set. Note: May substitute ½ t. cinnamon, ¼ t. ginger and ⅛ t. cloves in place of pumpkin pie spice.

tips and hints

WITHOUT FRIENDS, LIFE WOULD BE LIKE A GARDEN

WITHOUT FLOWERS.

MRS. HENRY (ALMA) MAST

NOTES

Cakes, Cookies & Frostings

Four layers high for a wedding cake,
Six cake mixes you need to bake.
With a hexagon shape and pure white,
And plenty of roses, it looked just right!

On Wednesday eve into the "eck" it was set,
With orders to keep all hands off, you can bet!
Come Thursday morn, it still looked pretty as ever;
Those tiny dewdrops on the roses made it look clever!

It was cut into pieces after lunch,
Enough to serve a whole bunch.
We told everyone who had a part to get a piece;
Take it along home to enjoy it, if you please!

The pretty roses on top, no one did taste,
But I'd really hate to see them go to waste,
So we took them off and stored them away,
To bring back memories, many a day!

*A*fter lunch Aden and I, with help from the witnesses, cut the wedding cake and put the slices in sandwich bags. At the supper table the cake slices were passed around and everyone who had a part got to take a slice home. We had enough left to enjoy for several days after the wedding.

Aden and Miriam
October 2, 2003

Jelly Roll

4 eggs, separated
¾ c. white sugar
¾ c. bread flour
1 t. baking powder
¼ t. salt
1 t. vanilla

Filling:
2 c. flour
4½ c. brown sugar
6 c. hot water
½ c. butter
2 t. maple flavoring

Beat egg yolks well; add sugar, flour, baking powder, salt and vanilla. Last add well-beaten egg whites. Bake at 400° for 13 minutes. For filling, combine first three ingredients and heat until thick, stirring constantly. Remove from heat and add butter and maple flavoring.

Mom cooked 6 batches of filling on Monday, but ended up making 3 more Tuesday evening when we made the jelly rolls. We made a total of 35 and only 3 of them flopped. We ate the flopped ones for a snack that evening. We served jelly rolls for dinner and supper and still had a nice amount left.

Angel Food Cake

1¼ c. cake flour
1¼ c. powdered sugar
2 c. egg whites
2 t. cream of tartar

1 t. vanilla
¼ t. salt
1 c. sugar

Sift together flour and powdered sugar. Beat egg whites, cream of tartar, vanilla and salt. Add sugar. Bake at 425° for ½ hour.

Levi & Mary Miller

Mexican Chocolate Chiffon

¾ c. hot coffee
⅓ c. cocoa
1¾ c. flour
1⅔ c. sugar
½ t. salt
1½ t. soda

½ c. vegetable oil
7 egg yolks
2 t. vanilla
7 egg whites
½ t. cream of tartar

Mix coffee and cocoa; let cool. Sift together flour, sugar, salt and soda. Add to coffee and cocoa. Add next three ingredients. Beat egg whites and cream of tartar. Add to rest of ingredients. Bake in an angel food cake pan.

Levi & Mary Miller

Chiffon Cake

2$\frac{1}{4}$ c. flour
1$\frac{1}{2}$ c. sugar
1 T. baking powder
1 t. salt
$\frac{1}{2}$ c. salad oil

6 eggs, separated
$\frac{3}{4}$ c. water
2 t. vanilla
$\frac{1}{2}$ t. cream of tartar

Sift together first 4 ingredients. Mix together oil, egg yolks, water and vanilla. Add to flour mixture. Beat egg whites and cream of tartar until stiff and add to rest of ingredients. Bake in an angel food cake pan.

Levi & Mary Miller

Wedding Cake Frosting

4 c. powdered sugar
$\frac{3}{4}$ c. Crisco
4 T. water

$\frac{1}{2}$ t. salt
$\frac{1}{4}$ t. orange flavoring
1 T. vanilla

Mix all together. The more you mix, the fluffier it gets.

I take this recipe times seven for an average wedding cake. It takes around 10 lb. powdered sugar and that means a lot of beating! Close to 40 roses are made a few days in advance, so they are dried and can be handled.

Mary C. Miller

Wooden Spoon Wedding Cookbook   **103**

CAKES, COOKIES & FROSTINGS

MY CHOCOLATE CAKE

2 c. brown sugar	2$^1/_4$ c. cake flour
$^1/_2$ c. oleo	2 t. soda
2 eggs	$^1/_2$ t. salt
$^1/_2$ c. sour cream	1 t. vanilla
4 T. cocoa	1 c. hot water

Cream together brown sugar, oleo and eggs. Add sour cream. Sift dry ingredients together and add to creamed mixture. Add vanilla and hot water. Mix well. Pour into greased 9" x 13" pan. Bake at 350° for 35 minutes.

Mrs. Crist (Verba) Miller

ONE-BOWL CHOCOLATE CAKE

2 c. flour	$^1/_2$ t. salt
2 c. sugar	1 c. vegetable oil
$^1/_2$ c. baking cocoa	1 c. milk or buttermilk
2 t. baking soda	2 eggs
1 t. baking powder	1 c. hot water

In a large bowl combine dry ingredients. Stir in oil, milk and eggs. Add water and stir until combined. Pour into a greased 13" x 9" pan. Bake at 350° for 35-38 minutes or until a toothpick near center comes out clean.

Mrs. Ervin (Mary) Byler

tips and hints

SLIP YOUR HAND INSIDE A WAXED SANDWICH BAG

AND YOU HAVE A PERFECT MITT FOR GREASING

BAKING PANS AND CASSEROLE DISHES.

EMMA MILLER

MY FAVORITE CHOCOLATE CAKE

2 c. white sugar	1 t. baking powder
2 eggs	2 t. soda
1 c. sour milk	1 t. vanilla
$2/3$ c. cocoa	1 c. brewed coffee
1 c. shortening	3 c. flour
pinch of salt	

Put ingredients in a bowl in order given. Beat all together for $1^{1}/_{2}$ minutes, or 150 to 200 beats by spoon. Bake at 350° for 30-35 minutes.

This is one of the first cakes I made when I was learning to bake. More than once I made a mistake while making it, but I don't remember that it ever flopped. I was 12 years old when my youngest sister was born. While Mom was at the birthing center I made this cake all by myself. Mom was surprised when she got home, as I had never baked it before without her help.

LAZY WIFE CAKE

$1^{1}/_{2}$ c. pastry flour	3 T. cocoa
$1/4$ t. salt	1 c. white sugar
2 t. soda	7 T. cooking oil
1 t. vanilla	1 T. vinegar

Mix all the dry ingredients together. Sift with a fork. Make three holes in it. Into one put the vanilla, the next the oil, and into the third put the vinegar. Pour 1 c. cold water over all this. Mix together just until mixed. Don't overbeat. Bake at 350° for 25-30 minutes or until done. Use a 9" x 9" ungreased cake pan.

Mrs. Andy (Lizzie) Miller

Respect is love in plain clothes.

Wooden Spoon Wedding Cookbook **105**

LAZY WOMAN'S CAKE

3 c. all-purpose flour
1 1/2 c. white sugar
6 T. cocoa
2 t. salt

2 t. soda
1 T. vanilla
2 T. vinegar
3/4 c. oil

Sift dry ingredients together in a bowl. Make three holes. In one hole put vanilla, in one hole put vinegar, and in one hole put oil. Pour 2 c. cold water over this. Mix well. Pour into ungreased 9" x 13" x 2" pan. Bake at 350° for 30 minutes or a little more.

Mrs. John (Katie) Troyer

FLUFFY WHITE CAKE

2 c. sugar
1/2 c. shortening
1 c. lukewarm water
2 1/2 c. flour

4 t. baking powder
1 t. vanilla
4 egg whites, beaten

Mix together, adding beaten egg whites last. Pour into a greased 13" x 9" x 2" pan. Bake at 350°.

tips and hints

WHEN STRAWBERRIES ARE IN SEASON BE SURE TO MAKE
PANCAKES. SPOON STRAWBERRIES OVER PANCAKES AND ADD
A DOLLOP OF WHIPPED CREAM INSTEAD OF MAPLE SYRUP.

SPONGE CAKE

2 c. brown sugar
2 eggs
1 c. sour cream and
   1 c. sweet milk or
   1 c. sweet cream and
   1 c. buttermilk
2 t. soda

2 t. baking powder
$1/2$ t. salt
3 c. flour
1 t. cloves
1 t. cinnamon or
   1 t. black walnut extract
1 t. vanilla

Mix all together and pour into 9" x 13" pan and bake at 350°.

Mrs. Jacob (Esther) Miller

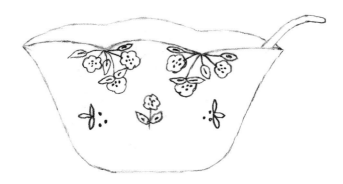

I received this punch bowl set for Christmas from Aden. After we had cut the wedding cake we put the punch bowl, filled with punch, in the "eck" where the cake had been.

CAKES, COOKIES & FROSTINGS

CARAMEL CAKE

2 c. brown sugar	2 eggs
$^1/_2$ c. butter	1 c. sour milk
1 T. peanut butter	1 t. soda
1 T. cocoa	2$^1/_2$ c. flour

Cream sugar and butter together. Add rest of ingredients. Bake at 350°.
Delicious with peanut butter icing!

Miriam Miller

ZUCCHINI CAKE

$^3/_4$ c. vegetable oil	$^1/_2$ t. baking powder
1$^3/_4$ c. white sugar	1 t. soda
2 eggs	$^1/_2$ t. cinnamon
1 t. vanilla	$^1/_2$ t. cloves
$^1/_2$ c. sour milk	2 c. finely chopped zucchini
2$^1/_2$ c. unsifted flour	$^1/_4$ c. nuts, optional

Mix all ingredients together except zucchini. Stir zucchini in last. Pour into
greased 9" x 13" pan. Bake at 325° for 40-50 minutes.

Mrs. Henry D. (Alma) Mast

ZUCCHINI SQUASH CAKE

1/4 c. soft oleo
1/2 c. vegetable oil
1 3/4 c. white sugar
2 eggs
1 t. vanilla
1/2 c. sour milk
2 1/2 c. unsifted flour
4 t. cocoa
1/2 t. baking powder
1 t. soda
1/2 t. cinnamon
1/2 t. cloves
2 c. finely chopped zucchini
1/4 c. chocolate chips
1/4 c. chopped nuts

Mix all ingredients together except last three. Stir in zucchini and pour into ungreased pan. Sprinkle with chocolate chips and nuts. Bake at 325° for 40-50 minutes.

Mrs. David (Anna) Miller

Respect is what we owe; love is what we give.

BEFORE POURING CAKE BATTER INTO PAN, GREASE PAN WITH VEGETABLE OIL, THEN COAT WITH SUGAR. YOU SHOULD HAVE NO PROBLEM GETTING THE CAKE OUT OF THE PAN AS THE SUGAR KEEPS IT FROM STICKING.

Six cake mixes are used for an average wedding cake. The cake is four layers high, with a cardboard between the second and third layer to keep the weight a little more evenly divided. The cake was delivered the evening before the wedding. Aden and I carried it to the "eck" in case it was dropped. That way it would have been our own fault, but luckily it didn't happen.

POPPY SEED CHIFFON CAKE

2¹/₂ c. all-purpose flour
1 c. sugar
1 T. baking powder
¹/₂ t. salt
³/₄ c. water
¹/₂ c. vegetable oil

5 egg yolks
1 t. lemon extract
1 t. grated lemon peel
1 (12¹/₂ oz.) can poppy seed filling
7 egg whites, room temperature
¹/₂ t. cream of tartar

Lemon Butter Frosting:
6 T. butter, softened
4 c. powdered sugar
3-5 T. milk

1 T. lemon juice
1 t. lemon extract

In a mixing bowl, combine flour, sugar, baking powder and salt. Add water, oil, egg yolks, lemon extract, lemon peel and filling; beat until smooth. In another bowl, beat egg whites and cream of tartar until stiff peaks form. Fold into batter; pour into a 10" tube pan. Bake at 350° for 55-60 minutes or until cake springs back when lightly touched. Invert pan on a bottle; cool completely. Remove cake from pan. For frosting, cream butter and sugar in a bowl. Add milk, lemon juice and extract; beat until smooth. Frost cake. Serves 12-16 people. If you don't have poppy seed filling, use ¹/₂ c. poppy seeds and ¹/₄ c. extra water.

Mrs. Menno D. Schmucker

SUGAR PLUM SPICE CAKE

2¹/₂ c. flour	³/₄ t. salt
1 t. soda	³/₄ t. cinnamon
³/₄ t. cloves	¹/₂ c. vegetable oil
1 c. white sugar	2 eggs
²/₃ c. brown sugar	1¹/₄ c. sour milk
1 t. baking powder	

Mix together in order given and mix well. Bake at 350° for 30 minutes or until done. Very good with brown sugar icing.

Mrs. Levi (Mary) Miller

OATMEAL NUT CAKE

1 c. quick oats	1¹/₂ c. sifted flour
1¹/₄ c. boiling water	2 eggs
1 c. white sugar	1 t. soda
1 c. brown sugar	1 t. cinnamon
¹/₂ c. Wesson oil	¹/₂ t. salt

Topping:

1 c. brown sugar	6 T. melted butter
1 c. coconut	3 T. cream
1 c. nuts	

Bake cake at 350° until done, then spread with topping and put back in oven for 10 minutes or until bubbly.

Mrs. Mahlon (Katie) Miller

Every person who had a part in our wedding (which was around 70 people) received a thank-you card for their help. Aden and his sister Barbara helped me make them one evening, but I spent many evenings working on them alone. I enjoyed it, but was glad when they were done.

MOLASSES CAKE (SUGARLESS)

³/₄ c. canola oil
2 eggs, beaten
1 c. cane molasses
¹/₂ c. Karo, then fill cup with water
1¹/₂ c. sweet milk

1 T. baking soda
1 t. allspice
1 t. cinnamon
4 c. flour
1 c. brown sugar, optional

Beat eggs; add oil, Karo, soda and molasses. Beat again. Alternately add dry ingredients and milk. Pour batter into a 10" x 14" pan or 2 smaller pans and bake at 350° for 30 minutes.

Mrs. Atlee V. (Barbara) Wengerd

CREAM-FILLED COFFEE CAKE

1 T. yeast
¹/₂ c. warm water
1 c. milk
¹/₂ c. oleo

¹/₂ c. sugar
2 eggs
1 t. salt
3¹/₂ c. flour

Crumbs:
¹/₄ c. margarine
¹/₂ c. flour

¹/₂ c. brown sugar

Cream Filling:
1 c. Crisco
2 egg whites
3 c. powdered sugar

2 T. flour
4 T. milk
2 t. vanilla

Scald milk; cool to lukewarm. Add oleo, sugar and salt. Beat eggs; add milk mixture. Dissolve yeast in warm water and add. Mix in flour and let rise. Put in three 9" pans. Spread crumbs on top; let rise. Bake at 350°. Cool; cut cakes in half and spread cream filling between halves.

CREAM-FILLED COFFEE CAKE

2 1/2 c. all-purpose flour
1 c. brown sugar
1/2 c. white sugar
1/2 c. butter
1 egg, beaten

1 t. soda
1 t. baking powder
1/2 t. salt
1 t. vanilla
1 c. buttermilk or sour milk

Filling:
1/2 c. Crisco
1 c. marshmallow creme
2 c. powdered sugar

1 t. vanilla
enough milk for soft filling

Cream butter and sugars. Add flour, salt, soda and baking powder. Reserve 3/4 c. crumbs for topping. Add rest of ingredients to the rest of crumbs. Mix well. Spoon into 2 greased and floured pie pans. Add 1/2 t. cinnamon to the 3/4 c. crumbs and put on top of batter. Bake at 325° for 25 minutes or until toothpick comes out clean. Let cool, then split in half lengthwise and put filling in between.

Mrs. David D. (Emma) Miller

The best antique in life is…an old friend.

tips and hints

TO GET A CAKE TO RISE EVENLY, TAKE AN OLD TOWEL AND TEAR IT INTO A STRIP, WIDE ENOUGH TO FOLD IN HALF. WET THE TOWEL AND PUT AROUND THE CAKE PAN, PINNING THE ENDS TOGETHER, THEN BAKE.

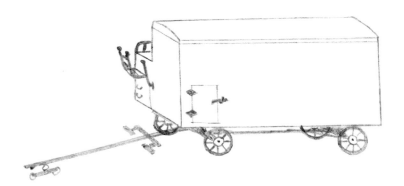

This is a typical bench wagon. Each church district has its own bench wagon. It is pulled by two horses from place to place wherever church is. It is filled with backless benches and enough dishes to be used for lunch at church. We borrowed the neighboring churches' bench wagons for our wedding, so we had three.

MY TRUE LOVE CAKE

1/2 c. butter, softened
2 c. sugar
2 eggs
1 t. vanilla
2 c. flour

3 T. plus 1 1/2 t. cocoa
1 t. soda
1/2 c. buttermilk
1 c. water
1/2 c. vegetable oil

Filling:
2 (8 oz.) pkg. cream cheese
2/3 c. sugar
1/4 c. whipped cream

1 (21 oz.) can cherry pie
filling, divided

Cream butter and sugar. Add eggs one at a time, beating well after each addition. Beat in oil and vanilla. Mix flour, cocoa and soda. Add alternately with buttermilk and water. Pour into greased and floured 9" heart-shaped pans. Bake at 350° for 20-25 minutes. Cool 10 minutes before removing from pans. For filling, beat cream cheese and sugar until fluffy. Beat in cream. Place one cake on serving plate; spread with half of cream cheese mixture. Refrigerate 10 minutes. Top with 1 c. pie filling and second cake; spread remaining cream cheese mixture. Make a heart-shaped indention in center of cake; fill with remaining pie filling.

tips and hints

PLACE ICE CREAM CONES IN A CUPCAKE PAN. FILL CONES
HALF FULL WITH CAKE BATTER. BAKE AT 350 DEGREES
FOR 20-25 MINUTES. COOL. FROST AND DECORATE.

Wooden Spoon Wedding Cookbook   117

HO-HO CAKE

1 chocolate cake mix or use Texas sheet cake

Filling:

5 T. flour	$^{1}/_{2}$ c. oleo
1$^{1}/_{4}$ c. milk	$^{1}/_{2}$ c. Crisco
1 c. sugar	

Topping:

$^{1}/_{2}$ c. oleo, melted	3 c. powdered sugar
3 T. cocoa	1 t. vanilla
2 T. hot water (more or less)	1 egg, beaten

Cook flour and milk until thick. Combine sugar, oleo and Crisco until fluffy, then add to flour mixture. Spread over cake. Mix topping ingredients together and spread over white layer. Do not pour topping on until white layer is set. Don't mix topping until ready to use. Pour.

Mrs. David (Anna) Miller

DUMP CAKE

1 can crushed pineapple with juice	1 yellow cake mix
1 can cherry pie filling	1 c. butter

Dump cherry pie filling and pineapple in a 9" x 13" cake pan. Spread evenly in pan. Dump cake mix evenly on top of fruit. Cut butter in $^{1}/_{4}$" squares and spread it over cake mix. Bake at 375° for 35-50 minutes or until crust is brown. Very good served warm with ice cream.

CHECKER BOARD CAKE

White Batter:
1 c. sugar
1/2 c. butter
1/2 c. water
2 c. pastry flour
1 t. vanilla
4 egg whites, beaten with
   1/4 c. white sugar

Chocolate Batter:
1 c. brown sugar
1/2 c. butter
1/2 c. water
4 egg yolks
2 c. pastry flour
2 t. baking powder
2 T. cocoa
1 t. vanilla

Use three 8" round pans or one 10" x 13" pan. Pour white batter in pan. Pour chocolate batter on top and marbleize with knife. Bake at 350° for approximately 40 minutes, or until it tests done. As a girl growing up, this was a favorite cake.

Emma Miller

Promptness—when stern duty calls; courage—when adversity falls.

tips and hints

WHEN SOWING CARROTS ADD A FEW RADISH SEEDS. THE RADISHES COME UP BEFORE THE CARROTS, SO YOU CAN SEE YOUR ROW SOONER.

TRIPLE-LAYER MOCHA CAKE

1 c. shortening	3 c. flour
2¹/₂ c. sugar	4 t. cocoa
5 eggs, separated	1 t. soda
5 T. strong brewed coffee	¹/₂ t. salt
2 t. vanilla	1 c. buttermilk

Frosting:

5¹/₂-6 c. powdered sugar	1¹/₂ t. vanilla
1 T. cocoa	3 T. plus 1¹/₂ t. strong brewed coffee
1¹/₂ c. butter, softened	

Cream shortening and sugar. Add egg yolks, one at a time, beating well after each addition. Beat in coffee and vanilla. Combine dry ingredients; add to the creamed mixture alternately with buttermilk. In another bowl, beat egg whites until stiff peaks form; fold into batter. Pour into 3 greased and floured 9" baking pans. Bake at 350° for 25-30 minutes or until a toothpick inserted near the center comes out clean. Cool for 10 minutes before removing from pans. For frosting, combine powdered sugar and cocoa. Add butter and stir well before adding coffee and vanilla. Spread between layers and over top and sides of cake. Serves 12-14 people.

With sewing for a family of seven, you can imagine Mom has a lot of material scraps. And that is probably what gave us the idea to give these hand towels to the cooks for thank-you gifts. We had 30 cooks, so that means 30 hand towels were sewn. We bought the dish towels, then sewed on the top so it can be hung at the sink. Each cook also received a casserole dish.

CAKES, COOKIES & FROSTINGS

FIVE-FLAVOR POUND CAKE

3 c. sugar
$1/2$ c. margarine
1 c. Crisco
6 eggs
1 c. milk
1 T. baking powder

3 c. flour
1 t. vanilla flavoring
1 t. lemon flavoring
1 t. orange flavoring
1 t. coconut flavoring
1 t. pineapple flavoring

Glaze:
1 c. sugar
$1/2$ c. margarine

$1/2$ c. water
$1/2$ t. of each flavoring

Cream Crisco, margarine and sugar; add rest of ingredients. Pour in ungreased tube pan and bake at 350° for one hour. Combine glaze ingredients; cook until it strings. Aden does not care for coconut, so I substitute coconut flavoring with banana, though I think the original is still the best.

ANGEL FOOD CAKE

14 egg whites
$1^1/2$ c. white sugar
1 t. cream of tartar

1 heaping c. Flaky Crust flour
pinch of salt

Beat eggs lightly. Add salt and cream of tartar. Beat stiff; fold in sugar, then add flour; add 2 T. cold water. Pour into an angel food cake pan and bake at 350° for 1 hour. For chocolate cake add $1/4$ c. cocoa and only $3/4$ c. flour.

Mrs. John (Fannie) Miller

122 *Wooden Spoon Wedding Cookbook*

ANGEL FOOD JELLY ROLL

1 angel food cake
pie filling

whipped topping

Bake an angel food cake in two cookie sheets. When cooled fill with pie filling with a little whipped topping added and roll up into a jelly roll.

JELLY ROLL

5 eggs, separated
$^{1}/_{2}$ t. cream of tartar
1 c. sugar
1 t. vanilla

1 c. flour
1 t. baking powder
$^{1}/_{4}$ t. salt

Separate eggs. Beat egg whites and cream of tartar until it stands in peaks. Slowly beat in sugar. Beat yolks with fork and add to egg whites. Add sifted flour, baking powder, salt and vanilla. Put wax paper in pan to bake them, then once they are done just roll wax paper along with jelly roll until cold. Unroll. Spread filling on top, then remove paper and roll again. Bake at 375°. Yield: 1 roll.

Mrs. Dan J. (Mary) Miller

Love is willing to be inconvenienced.

COWBOY COFFEE CAKE

3 c. flour	$^{1}/_{2}$ t. soda
2 c. brown sugar	$^{1}/_{2}$ t. cinnamon
$^{1}/_{2}$ t. salt	$^{1}/_{2}$ t. nutmeg
$^{1}/_{2}$ c. shortening	1 c. sour milk
2 t. baking powder	2 well-beaten eggs

Mix flour, sugar, salt and shortening together until crumbly, then reserve
$^{3}/_{4}$ c. crumbs. Mix rest of ingredients together and pour in 9" x 13" pan,
then put reserved crumbs on top. Bake at 350°. Also very delicious served
warm with hot chocolate or fruit and milk.

I started to make this cake the first year we were married and it has been
a favorite since. The children used to look forward to a day with Dad
when I was away. Dad would bake this cake for lunch and serve it
with hot chocolate.

Mrs. Jacob (Esther) Miller

CRUMB CAKE

2 c. brown sugar	1 c. sour milk or buttermilk
$^{1}/_{2}$ c. shortening	1 t. soda
$2^{1}/_{2}$ c. flour	1 t. allspice
1 egg	pinch of salt

Mix sugar, shortening and flour like pie dough, nice and fine. Take out $^{3}/_{4}$
c. crumbs. To the rest of the crumbs add the rest of the ingredients. Put in
a loaf pan and spread rest of crumbs on top of batter. Bake at 325°.

Elmina Miller

CAKES, COOKIES & FROSTINGS

SHORTCAKE

2 c. flour	**$^1/_4$ c. oleo**
$^1/_3$ c. sugar	**1 egg**
4 t. baking powder	**$^1/_3$ c. milk**
$^1/_2$ t. salt	

Mix and put into 9" x 9" baking pan. Bake at 350° for 15 minutes. Serve warm, topped with your favorite fruit and milk.

SHORTCAKE

2 c. sifted flour	**6 T. butter**
2 t. baking powder	**1 egg, well beaten**
$^3/_4$ t. salt	**$^1/_2$ c. milk**
$^1/_2$ c. sugar	

Bake at 375° for 25-30 minutes.

Topping:

$1^1/_2$ T. butter, melted	**1 T. flour**
4 T. brown sugar	**$^1/_2$ t. cinnamon**

Brush top with melted butter, then sift on the sugar, flour and cinnamon.

Elmina Miller

Loves makes it possible to believe the impossible.

BLUEBERRY MUFFINS

2 c. flour	1 c. milk
$^2/_3$ c. sugar	$^1/_3$ c. butter, melted
1 T. baking powder	1 t. nutmeg
$^1/_2$ t. salt	1 t. vanilla
eggs	2 c. fresh or frozen blueberries

In a mixing bowl combine flour, sugar, baking powder and salt. In another bowl beat eggs. Blend in milk, butter, nutmeg and vanilla. Pour into dry ingredients and mix just until moistened. Fold in blueberries. Fill greased or paper-lined muffin cups $^2/_3$ full. Bake at 375° for 20-25 minutes. Brush tops with butter and sprinkle with sugar. Note: If using frozen blueberries, rinse and pat dry before adding to dough. Yield: 1 dozen.

MINI COFFEE CAKES

$^1/_3$ c. butter, softened	1 T. baking powder
$^1/_4$ c. sugar	$^1/_4$ t. salt
1 egg	$1^1/_4$ c. milk
$1^1/_2$ c. flour	$^1/_2$ c. chopped walnuts
1 pkg. vanilla instant pudding	

Topping:

$^1/_2$ c. chopped walnuts	2 T. butter, melted
$^1/_3$ c. packed brown sugar	$^1/_4$ t. cinnamon

In a mixing bowl cream butter and sugar. Beat in egg. Combine flour, pudding mix, baking powder and salt. Add to the creamed mixture alternately with milk. Beat until blended. Stir in walnuts. Fill paper-lined muffin cups two-thirds full. Combine topping ingredients; sprinkle over batter. Bake at 375° for 20-25 minutes or until toothpick inserted near center comes out clean. Yield: approximately 1 dozen.

FROSTED PUMPKIN GEMS

1 (15 oz.) can solid pack pumpkin
3 eggs
$^1/_2$ c. vegetable oil

2 t. cinnamon
1 t. soda
1 yellow cake mix

Mix all ingredients, adding pumpkin last. Pour into 24 paper-lined cupcakes. Bake at 350° for 12-16 minutes or until a toothpick inserted near the center comes out clean. Frost with cream cheese frosting.

The first year we planted a garden after we were married, we planted two pumpkin plants, since Aden is fond of pumpkin bars. Much to our surprise, we got 33 pumpkins from those two plants. So I tried out some new pumpkin recipes and this one became a favorite.

PUMPKIN BARS

2 c. brown sugar
2 eggs, beaten
$^1/_2$ c. oil
1 c. pumpkin
1 c. nuts

2 c. flour
$^1/_2$ t. salt
2 t. cinnamon
1 t. soda
1 t. baking powder

Frosting:
$3^1/_2$ c. powdered sugar
3 oz. cream cheese
6 T. melted butter

1 t. vanilla
milk

Mix together and pour into a 9" x 13" x 2" cookie sheet and bake at 350°. Cool; frost.

Wooden Spoon Wedding Cookbook   127

If you go up and down several hills and around a few curves on Township Road 654, you will eventually come to a newly built home that resembles this house and barn. We had carpenters come in and build the house, but Aden did the barn with help from relatives and neighbors.

FRESH APPLE BARS

3 eggs
1 c. cooking oil
1³/₄ c. white sugar
2 c. all-purpose flour
¹/₂ t. salt

¹/₂ t. cinnamon
1 t. soda
2 c. finely chopped fresh apples
1 c. chopped nuts

Beat the first 3 ingredients well, then add the rest. Pour into a large cookie sheet. Bake at 350°.

Mrs. Emanuel R. (Fannie) Coblentz

LUSCIOUS LEMON BARS

¹/₄ c. butter, softened
2 T. powdered sugar

¹/₂ c. flour

Filling:
1 egg
¹/₂ c. sugar
2 T. lemon juice

1 T. flour
¹/₈ t. baking powder

Cream butter and powdered sugar; gradually beat in flour. Press into an ungreased 8" x 4" loaf pan. Bake at 325° for 14-16 minutes or until set and edges are lightly browned. For filling, beat together all the ingredients until frothy. Pour over warm crust. Bake for 18-22 minutes or until lightly browned. Dust with powdered sugar.

DOUBLE-DECKER BROWNIES

³/₄ c. butter
1 c. white sugar
1 c. brown sugar
3 large eggs, beaten
1 t. vanilla
2¹/₄ c. flour

2¹/₂ t. baking powder
¹/₂ t. salt
¹/₃ c. cocoa
1 T. butter
1 c. M&Ms
¹/₄ c. flour

Cream ³/₄ c. butter and sugars until light and fluffy. Add eggs, vanilla, baking powder, salt and flour. Mix well, then divide batter in half. Melt 1 T. butter and cocoa together, then mix into one part of dough. Spread evenly into 13" x 9" x 2" pan. Stir ¹/₄ c. flour and ¹/₂ c. M&Ms into other half of dough and spread over cocoa part in pan. Sprinkle with remaining ¹/₂ c. M&Ms. Bake 25-30 minutes in 350° oven.

Martha A. Miller

4-LAYER BARS

1 cake mix
¹/₂ c. butter, melted
1 egg

3 c. colored mini marshmallows
1 c. M&Ms
¹/₂ c. chopped walnuts or peanuts

Mix cake mix, butter and egg until well blended. Spread onto bottom of lightly greased 13" x 9" pan. Bake at 375° for 16-20 minutes. Sprinkle marshmallows, M&Ms and nuts over cake. Bake an additional 2-3 minutes or until marshmallows begin to puff. Cool completely. Cut into bars. Spray knife with nonstick cooking spray before cutting into bars.

CANDY-TOPPED BARS

2 c. flour
$^2/_3$ c. packed brown sugar
1 c. cold butter
1 c. chopped pecans
2 (8 oz.) pkg. cream cheese,
   softened

$^1/_2$ c. sugar
2 eggs
4 T. milk
2 T. lemon juice
1 t. vanilla extract
1-2 c. baking M&Ms

Combine flour and brown sugar. Cut in butter until mixture resembles coarse crumbs. Stir in pecans. Set aside 1 c. for topping. Press remaining crumbs into greased 9" x 13" pan. Bake at 350° for 12-15 minutes or until edges are lightly browned. Beat cream cheese and sugar. Add eggs, milk, lemon juice and vanilla; mix well. Pour over warm crust. Sprinkle with reserved crumb mixture. Bake for 25-30 minutes or until set. Immediately sprinkle with M&Ms. Cool; cut into bars.

BUTTERSCOTCH FUDGE BARS

$^1/_2$ c. butter
1 square (1 oz.) unsweetened
   chocolate
$^2/_3$ c. packed brown sugar
1 egg

1 t. vanilla
1 c. flour
1 t. baking powder
dash of salt
1 c. butterscotch chips

Melt butter and chocolate. Remove from heat; stir in brown sugar until dissolved. Cool to lukewarm. Add egg and vanilla; mix well. Combine the flour, baking powder and salt; stir into chocolate mixture until blended. Stir in chips. Spread in a greased 9" square baking pan. Bake at 350° for 22-27 minutes or until toothpick comes out with moist crumbs.

CAKES, COOKIES & FROSTINGS

MISSISSIPPI MUD BARS

1 c. melted oleo	$^1/_3$ c. cocoa
2 c. white sugar	$1^1/_2$ c. nuts
4 eggs	1 t. vanilla
$1^1/_2$ c. flour	1 t. baking powder

Icing:

$^1/_4$ c. oleo	$3^3/_4$ c. powdered sugar
$^1/_3$ c. milk	$^1/_3$ c. cocoa
1 t. vanilla	

Mix together thoroughly. Pour into greased and floured 13" x 9" cookie sheet. Bake at 350° for 30 minutes. While cake is hot spread with 9 oz. marshmallow creme. Have icing ready to spread over marshmallow creme.

FUDGE NUT BARS

1 c. butter	1 t. soda
2 c. brown sugar	1 t. salt
2 eggs	2 c. rolled oats
2 t. vanilla	2 c. flour

Filling:

2 c. chocolate chips	2 t. vanilla
1 can Eagle Brand milk	$^1/_2$ t. salt
1 c. nuts	

Mix dough and spread in a 13" x 9" cookie sheet. Reserve some dough to put on top. For filling, put milk, chips and salt in a saucepan. Put on low heat. Mix until melted and smooth; stir in nuts and vanilla; spread over dough. Dot remainder of dough over filling. Bake at 350° for 25-30 minutes.

CHOCOLATE MARSHMALLOW BARS

$^1/_2$ c. oleo	2 c. flour
1 c. brown sugar	$^1/_2$ t. soda
1 egg	$^1/_2$ t. salt
1 t. vanilla	$^1/_2$ c. milk
$^1/_4$ c. cocoa	miniature marshmallows

Icing:

$^1/_3$ c. butter	2 T. cocoa
1 c. brown sugar	$^1/_4$ c. milk

Combine sugar, oleo, egg and vanilla. Add dry ingredients and milk. Spread on greased cookie sheet. Bake at 375° for 8 minutes. Remove from oven and sprinkle marshmallows over top. Return to oven for 1 minute. For icing, combine and boil until it forms large bubbles; cool. Add powdered sugar to thicken. Spread thinly over bars.

Mrs. Aden (Dora) Miller

DISAPPEARING MARSHMALLOW BROWNIES

1 c. butterscotch chips	$^1/_2$ t. salt
$^1/_2$ c. butter	1 t. vanilla
$1^1/_2$ c. flour	2 eggs
$^2/_3$ c. brown sugar	2 c. miniature marshmallows
2 t. baking powder	2 c. chocolate chips

Melt butterscotch chips and butter; cool to lukewarm. Add flour, brown sugar, baking powder, salt, vanilla and eggs. Mix well. Add marshmallows and chocolate chips. Spread in a greased 9" x 13" pan. Bake at 350° for 20-25 minutes. Center will be jiggly but becomes firm when cool.

CHOCOLATE CHIP BARS

1½ c. packed brown sugar
½ c. butter, melted (no substitutes)
2 eggs, beaten
1 t. vanilla

1½ c. flour
½ t. baking powder
½ t. salt
1 c. chocolate chips

In a large bowl combine brown sugar, butter, eggs and vanilla just until blended. Combine flour, baking powder and salt; add to brown sugar mixture. Stir in chocolate chips. Spread into a greased 13" x 9" pan. Bake at 350° for 18-20 minutes or until a toothpick inserted near the center comes out clean. Cool. Cut in bars. Yield: 3 dozen.

Mrs. Ervin (Mary) Byler

CAN'T LEAVE ALONE BARS

1 white or yellow cake mix
2 eggs
⅓ c. oil

¼ c. butter
1 c. chocolate chips
1 can sweetened condensed milk

Mix cake mix, eggs and oil. Reserve 1 cup. Pat rest of mixture into bottom of 9" x 13" pan. Melt butter, chocolate chips and milk. Spread evenly on top of mixture, then put rest of dough on top. Bake at 350°. Cut in squares when cool.

Mrs. Crist (Verba) Miller

tips and hints

FRESH APPLES FLOAT BECAUSE 25% OF THEIR

VOLUME IS AIR.

PEANUT BUTTER DREAM BARS

2¹/₄ c. flour
3 c. oatmeal
1¹/₂ c. brown sugar
1¹/₂ t. soda
1 t. salt

1¹/₂ c. butter, melted
¹/₃ c. peanut butter
1 can Eagle Brand milk
¹/₂ c. baking M&M's
¹/₂ c. chocolate chips

Mix together flour, oatmeal, brown sugar, soda, salt and butter like crumbs. Save 1¹/₂ cups. Press the rest in a 9" x 13" cookie sheet. Bake for 10 minutes at 375°. Mix together peanut butter and Eagle Brand milk. Spread over crust. Sprinkle the rest of the crumbs, M&Ms and chocolate chips over the top. Bake 20 minutes more.

PEANUT BUTTER BARS

¹/₂ c. shortening, softened
¹/₂ c. white sugar
¹/₂ c. brown sugar
¹/₂ c. creamy peanut butter
1 egg
1 c. chocolate chips

1 t. vanilla
1 c. flour
¹/₂ c. quick oats
1 t. baking powder
¹/₄ t. salt

Mix all ingredients together except chocolate chips. Spread in greased 13" x 9" x 2" pan. Sprinkle chocolate chips on top. Bake at 350° for 20 to 25 minutes.

Wooden Spoon Wedding Cookbook   135

CAKES, COOKIES & FROSTINGS

BROWN SUGAR SHORTBREAD

**1 c. butter, softened (no
   substitutes)**

**$^1/_2$ c. packed brown sugar
2$^1/_4$ c. flour**

Cream butter and sugar. Gradually stir in flour. Turn onto a lightly floured
surface and knead until smooth, about 3 minutes. Pat into a $^1/_3$" thick
rectangle measuring 11" x 8". Cut into 2" x 1" strips. Place 1" apart on
ungreased baking sheets. Prick with a fork. Bake at 300° for 25 minutes or
until bottom begins to brown. Cool for 5 minutes before removing from
pan.

SOFT BATCH COOKIES

**1 c. white sugar
1 c. brown sugar
6 T. oleo
$^1/_4$ c. applesauce
2 eggs**

**3 c. flour
1$^1/_2$ t. soda
1 t. salt
2 c. chocolate chips**

The dough will be very dry. Bake at 350°. Do not overbake for a soft cookie.
This is my favorite cookie recipe, but I've had a problem to get them soft.
So I changed the recipe a bit. It is important not to overbake them.

tips and hints

ADD SOME VINEGAR IN CANNER WHEN COLD

PACKING MEATS.

KEEPS JARS FROM GETTING SO GREASY.

MRS. DAVID (ANNA) MILLER

136 *Wooden Spoon Wedding Cookbook*

MOM'S SOFT CHOCOLATE CHIP COOKIES

2 c. flour
1 t. soda in 1 drop water
1 c. brown sugar
$^1/_2$ c. shortening

1 t. vanilla
1 egg
8 oz. chocolate chips
4 oz. nuts

Bake at 350°. Do not overbake and they will be soft. This is one of the recipes Aden asked me to get from his mom, as it was one of his many favorites.

CHOCOLATE CHIP SANDWICH COOKIES

1 c. butter
$^3/_4$ c. white sugar
$^3/_4$ c. brown sugar
2 eggs
1 t. vanilla

1 t. soda
1 t. salt
2 c. chocolate chips
1 c. chopped nuts
$2^3/_4$ c. flour

Drop and flatten. Bake at 375° for 8 minutes or until lightly browned. Fill with whoopie pie filling.

Filling:
2 egg whites, beaten
1 t. cream of tartar
2 c. powdered sugar
1 T. vanilla or maple flavoring

2 T. flour
$^1/_2$ c. Crisco
$^3/_4$ c. marshmallow topping

Beat first five ingredients well; add Crisco and marshmallow topping. Cream until smooth. Fill two cookies sandwich style.

Erma Miller

CHOCOLATE CHIP COOKIES

1½ c. oleo
1 c. Crisco
1½ c. brown sugar
1½ c. white sugar
4 eggs
2 t. vanilla

1⅓ c. instant vanilla pudding
1 t. salt
2 t. soda
6 c. bread flour
3 c. chocolate chips

Mix together and drop by teaspoonsful onto greased cookie sheet. Bake at 375° until lightly browned. Do not overbake!

Mrs. Crist (Verba) Miller

ULTIMATE CHOCOLATE CHIP COOKIES

3 c. butter Crisco
5 c. brown sugar
4 eggs
8 T. milk
4 T. vanilla

4 t. salt
3 t. soda
7 c. Gold Medal flour
4 c. chocolate chips

Cream together Crisco and sugar. Add the eggs, milk, vanilla, salt and soda and beat well. Then add flour and chocolate chips and mix well. Bake at 325° for 12-15 minutes. Do not overbake; they should be soft when taken out of the oven.

Mrs. David D. (Emma) Miller

BEST CHOCOLATE CHIP COOKIES

1 c. white Crisco
2 c. brown sugar
2 eggs, beaten
$^{1}/_{2}$ t. salt
1 t. vanilla

3 t. baking powder
2 t. soda
chocolate chips, as desired
3 c. flour
nuts, optional

Mix in order given. Bake at 350° for 8-10 minutes. Do not overbake.
Though the recipe didn't say to sandwich these, we like them best that way.
I think the name is fitting.

tips and hints

ADD SEVERAL DROPS OF VINEGAR TO ICING WHILE

BEATING AND IT WILL BE SOFT AND SELDOM GRAINY.

EMMA MILLER

CAKES, COOKIES & FROSTINGS

CHOCOLATE DROP COOKIES

1 c. shortening	1 t. salt
2 c. brown sugar	1 t. soda
2 well-beaten eggs	1 c. cream, sweet milk or
2 t. vanilla	buttermilk
8 T. cocoa	1 c. nuts, if desired
3$^1/_3$ c. flour	

Cream shortening; add sugar, eggs and vanilla. Mix cocoa with flour. Blend well. Add dry ingredients with milk. Drop by teaspoonful. Bake at 350° for 10-12 minutes. Frost with Mocha Frosting while still warm.

Mocha Frosting:

4 T. cocoa	1 t. vanilla
6 T. hot coffee	3 c. powdered sugar
butter	

Combine coffee and cocoa. Add butter and vanilla; beat until smooth. Add sugar gradually until of spreading consistency.

Whenever Grandma (Davey Ella) baked cookies for someone for church, this is the kind she always made.

Miss Miriam Miller, Mrs. John (Katie) Miller

MOCHA WALNUT COOKIES

2 c. chocolate chips	$^1/_2$ c. butter, softened
2 t. instant coffee	$^1/_2$ c. white sugar
2 t. boiling water	$^1/_2$ c. brown sugar
$1^1/_4$ c. flour	1 egg
$^3/_4$ t. soda	$^1/_2$ c. chopped walnuts
$^1/_2$ t. salt	

Melt $^1/_2$ c. chocolate chips over hot water; stir until smooth. Cool to room temperature. In a small cup dissolve coffee in boiling water; set aside. In a small bowl combine flour, soda and salt. Set aside. In a large mixing bowl, combine butter, sugars and coffee. Beat until creamy. Add egg and melted chips; beat well. Gradually add flour mixture; stir in remaining $1^1/_2$ c. chocolate chips and walnuts. Drop on ungreased cookie sheet. Bake at 350° for 12 minutes. Allow to stand 2-3 minutes before removing from sheet. Yield: approximately 2 dozen 3" cookies.

CHEWY MOCHA KISSES

1 c. chocolate chips	1 t. instant coffee
2 eggs	$^1/_4$ t. vinegar
$^1/_8$ t. salt	$^1/_2$ c. coconut
sugar	$^1/_4$ c. chopped walnuts

Melt chocolate chips over hot water. Beat eggs and salt until foamy. Very gradually add sugar and beat until stiff peaks form. Add coffee and vinegar; beat well. Fold in coconut, walnuts and melted chocolate. Drop by teaspoonful onto greased cookie sheet and bake at 350° for 10 minutes.

A friend is someone who loves you, even when they know everything about you.

Many an hour was spent to make these nameplates which were set on the "eck" table. A nameplate was set at each setting with their name on it. We had one big one with "Aden and Miriam" on it instead of two separate names. Aden made the wooden part, I put the stain and varnish on it, and my cousin painted the names on the hummingbirds and also the date. Aden and I spent quite a few evenings helping each other put on the flowers. I would arrange them in bunches and he glued them in place. The morning before the wedding Aden glued the stones in place for a pathway, which put the finishing touch on!

FUDGY BROWNIE COOKIES

1 egg	$^1/_2$ c. flour
1 egg white	$^1/_2$ c. cocoa
1 c. sugar	$^1/_4$ t. baking powder
2 t. instant coffee granules	$^1/_4$ t. salt
1 T. boiling water	$^1/_4$ c. mini chocolate chips
$^1/_4$ c. butter, melted	$^1/_4$ c. chopped walnuts
1 T. light corn syrup	

Beat egg, egg white and sugar. Dissolve coffee granules in boiling water. Add coffee, butter and corn syrup to egg mixture; mix well. Add the rest of ingredients, adding chocolate chips last. Drop by tablespoonsful onto baking sheet. Bake at 350° for 10-12 minutes or until set. Note: The corn syrup and egg white keeps these cookies low fat.

S'MORE SANDWICH COOKIES

$^3/_4$ c. butter, softened	$1^1/_4$ c. all-purpose flour
$^1/_2$ c. white sugar	$1^1/_4$ c. graham cracker crumbs
$^1/_2$ c. packed brown sugar	$^1/_2$ t. baking soda
1 egg	$^1/_4$ t. salt
2 T. milk	$^1/_8$ t. cinnamon
1 t. vanilla	2 c. chocolate chips

In a mixing bowl, cream butter and sugars. Beat in egg, milk and vanilla. Combine the flour, graham cracker crumbs, soda, salt and cinnamon; gradually add to creamed mixture. Stir in chocolate chips. Drop by tablespoonsful 2 inches apart onto ungreased baking sheets. Bake at 375° for 8-10 minutes or until golden brown. Fill with whoopie filling.

Barbara Miller

TRILBY COOKIES

1 c. sugar
1 c. shortening
$^1/_2$ c. sour milk

2 c. flour
2 c. rolled oats
1 t. soda

Filling:
$^1/_2$ lb. dates
1 c. sugar

$^1/_2$ c. water

Mix all together and roll out dough. Bake at 350°. Cook filling together until thick.

Mrs. Jacob D. (Esther) Miller

OAT FILLED COOKIES

1 c. shortening
$1^1/_2$ c. brown sugar
2 eggs
$^1/_2$ t. salt

1 t. soda
1 t. vanilla
$2^1/_2$ c. flour
$1^1/_2$ c. oatmeal

Cream sugar and shortening; add eggs. Add the rest of ingredients. Drop by teaspoonsful, then flatten with the bottom of a wet glass.

Filling:
2 c. chopped dates
1 c. white sugar

1 c. water

Cook together approximately 10 minutes, then mash with potato masher until smooth.

Mrs. Dan J. (Mary) Miller

ROLLED OATS COOKIES

2 c. brown sugar
1 c. shortening
3 eggs
1 c. sour milk or buttermilk
2 c. rolled oats
3 c. flour

$^1/_2$ t. salt
1 t. cinnamon
1 t. baking powder
2 c. raisins
1 c. chopped nuts
1 t. baking soda

Blend all ingredients and drop by spoonsful onto ungreased cookie sheet.
Bake at 350° for 12-15 minutes.

Mrs. Atlee V. (Barbara) Wengerd

COCONUT OATMEAL COOKIES

2 c. shortening
2 c. brown sugar
2 c. white sugar
4 eggs
5 c. oatmeal
2 c. coconut

$3^1/_2$ c. flour
2 t. soda
2 t. baking powder
2 t. vanilla
1 c. nuts
1 pkg. chocolate chips, optional

Drop and bake at 375° for 8-10 minutes.

Emma Miller

Love makes the world go around, but cash pays the bills.

tips and hints

FOR GRANOLA OR SIMILAR CEREALS, TRY USING PEANUT

BUTTER INSTEAD OF SHORTENING. GIVES A PLEASANT,

DIFFERENT FLAVOR.

MRS. DAN (EMMA) MILLER

BUSHEL COOKIES

5 lb. brown sugar
12 eggs
2 lb. raisins
1 c. maple syrup
5 c. lard or butter
1 qt. sweet cream

2 lb. quick oatmeal
4 T. baking soda
4 T. baking powder
6 lb. flour
1 lb. salted peanuts

Chocolate chips are good too. They can be substituted for the raisins, or use half of each. Drop onto cookie sheets. Yield: approximately 300 cookies.

I remember the time when you had a carpenter crew coming in to do something, they would sleep at your place and you'd feed them three meals a day until they were done. Around 1975 we got a crew to build a shed for us. We baked a batch of these cookies and they ate them down to the last crumbs.

Mrs. Ivan A. Miller

BANANA COOKIES

2 c. oleo
4 c. brown sugar
3 c. mashed bananas
3 eggs
2 t. vanilla

8 c. flour
4 t. baking powder
4 t. soda
1 t. salt

Combine first 5 ingredients. Sift flour, baking powder, soda and salt together and add to first ingredients. Bake at 350°. Ice with your favorite icing.

Mrs. Jacob D. (Esther) Miller

PUMPKIN DROP COOKIES

½ c. shortening
3 c. sugar
1 (15 oz.) can pumpkin
2 eggs
½ c. milk
6 c. flour

2 t. soda
2 t. cinnamon
1 t. salt
1 t. allspice
½ t. cloves

Cream shortening and sugar. Beat in pumpkin, eggs and milk. Add flour, soda, salt and spices. Drop on greased cookie sheet and bake at 375° for 10-13 minutes. When cool frost with cream cheese frosting.

PUMPKIN WHOOPIE PIES

2 c. brown sugar
1½ c. pumpkin
1 t. vanilla
3¼ c. flour
1½ t. ginger
1 t. cloves

1 t. baking powder
1 t. salt
1 c. vegetable oil
2 eggs
1½ t. cinnamon
1 t. soda

Filling:
2 egg whites
½ c. Crisco

2 c. powdered sugar
1 t. vanilla

For filling, beat egg whites and add remaining ingredients.

Cindy Miller

PEANUT BUTTER COOKIES

$^1/_2$ c. butter, softened
$^1/_2$ c. white sugar
$^1/_2$ c. packed brown sugar
$^1/_2$ c. peanut butter
1 egg

$^1/_2$ t. vanilla
1$^1/_4$ c. flour
$^1/_2$ t. soda
$^1/_2$ t. baking powder

Cream butter and sugars. Add peanut butter, egg and vanilla; beat until smooth. Add flour, soda and baking powder; mix well. For easier shaping, chill the dough for 1 hour. Shape into balls; flatten each ball by crisscrossing with the tines of a fork dipped into sugar. Bake at 375° for 10-12 minutes.

PEANUT BUTTER COOKIES

1 c. white sugar
1 c. brown sugar
$^2/_3$ c. shortening
2 eggs, beaten
$^2/_3$ c. peanut butter

2$^3/_4$ c. flour
4 t. baking powder
$^1/_2$ t. soda
1 t. vanilla

Mix in order given. Roll in small balls. Place on cookie sheet. Flatten with fork both ways. Bake at 325°.

tips and hints

A STRAWBERRY IS THE ONLY FRUIT THAT HAS ITS

SEED ON THE OUTSIDE.

TRIPLE TREAT COOKIES

1 c. white sugar	3 c. flour, scant
1 c. brown sugar	1 c. peanut butter
1 c. oleo	2 t. baking soda
2 eggs	$1\frac{1}{2}$ t. salt
1 t. vanilla	$1\frac{1}{2}$ c. chocolate chips

Filling:

$\frac{1}{2}$ c. peanut butter	1 t. vanilla
$\frac{1}{3}$ c. milk	3 c. powdered sugar

Cream sugars, peanut butter, oleo and eggs. Add rest of ingredients and roll dough into balls. Bake at 350° for 8-10 minutes. Combine filling ingredients and put between cookies.

BUTTERSCOTCH COOKIES

6 c. brown sugar	1 T. salt
3 c. butter	1 T. vanilla
12 c. flour (2 c. bread flour)	1 T. soda
6 eggs, well beaten	1 T. cream of tartar

Cream butter and sugar; add vanilla and eggs. Sift remaining ingredients. Add and beat well. Make into rolls and let stand overnight. Slice and bake at 350° until done. Ice with your favorite icing.

Mrs. John D. (Katie) Miller

BUTTERSCOTCH CRUNCH SANDWICH COOKIES

2 c. shortening
2 c. brown sugar
2 c. white sugar
2 t. vanilla
4 eggs

3 c. flour
2 t. salt
2 t. soda
6 c. oatmeal
butterscotch chips

Filling:
$^1/_2$ c. butter
4 oz. cream cheese

$2^1/_2$ c. powdered sugar
maple flavoring

Mix well. Bake at 400° for 10 minutes. Do not overbake.

tips and hints

ACCORDING TO A STUDY, THE SCENT OF COFFEE AND
PEANUT BUTTER ARE THE TWO MOST RECOGNIZABLE
TO AMERICAN ADULTS.

CREAM WAFER COOKIES

1½ c. butter
3 c. brown sugar
5 eggs, beaten
8 c. Softex flour
1 T. soda

1 t. cinnamon
1 T. vanilla
1½ t. salt
5 T. cream

Cream butter and brown sugar. Add eggs; stir. Add soda, salt, vanilla, cinnamon and cream. Stir and add flour.

Frosting:
8 T. butter
4 c. powdered sugar
4 T. hot cream

vanilla to taste
salt to taste

One morning it was raining so Mom had to take the scholars to school in the buggy. Before she left, she told me to make four batches of cream wafer cookies, not realizing how many it would make. By the time Mom got back I had a 13 qt. mixing bowl almost full of cookie dough. I ended up using my hands to mix it. This has always been one of our favorite cookies and now everyone could eat to their hearts' content.

Mrs. Alvin (Ida) Miller, Verba Miller

A happy marriage is a union of two good forgivers.

CREAM WAFER COOKIES

1 c. shortening
2 c. brown sugar
4 eggs, beaten
1 t. vanilla

4 T. sweet cream
2 t. soda
2 t. baking powder
6 c. flour

Filling:
8 T. sweet cream
4 T. butter, melted

3 T. Crisco
powdered sugar

Mix. Press through cookie press. Bake until light brown. Cut into 3" pieces and immediately remove from cookie sheet. For filling, melt butter, then add cream and powdered sugar. When right spreading consistency, add Crisco and beat until smooth and fluffy. Spread between two cookies to form a sandwich. I use evaporated milk instead of sweet cream.

Mrs. Atlee V. (Barbara) Wengerd

SUGAR COOKIES

1 c. shortening
1 c. sugar
1 c. powdered sugar
1 c. vegetable oil
2 eggs

1 t. vanilla
4 c. flour
1 t. salt
1 t. soda
1 t. cream of tartar

Mix shortening until fluffy; add sugars, oil and eggs. Sift together flour, salt, soda and cream of tartar, and slowly add to mixture. Stir in vanilla. Roll into balls and flatten on ungreased cookie sheet, using the bottom of a glass dipped in sugar. Bake at 350° for 8-10 minutes. Do not overbake for a soft cookie. Good to sandwich.

CAKES, COOKIES & FROSTINGS

CARAMEL COOKIES

2 eggs
2 c. brown sugar
$^1/_2$ c. butter
$^1/_2$ c. lard
4 c. flour

2 T. hot water
2 t. soda
1 t. cream of tartar
1 t. vanilla

Make dough in the evening and form into a roll. Slice and bake the next morning. Bake at 350°.

Mrs. Mahlon (Katie) Miller

DANNY EMMA COOKIES

2 c. brown sugar
$^1/_2$ c. lard
1 T. water
2 t. vanilla

2 eggs
1 t. cream of tartar
3$^1/_2$ c. flour
2 tsp. soda

Make into rolls, then chill a few hours. Slice with thread. Note: I use half bread flour. An old-fashioned recipe, but one of Aden's favorites. We like them with or without frosting.

DEBBIE COOKIES

3 c. brown sugar
1½ c. oleo
4 eggs, beaten
1½ t. soda
1 t. salt

2 t. cinnamon
2 t. vanilla
2½ c. flour
4 c. oatmeal

Combine eggs, sugar and oleo; stir and add soda, salt, cinnamon and vanilla. Mix well; add flour and oatmeal. These cookies bake very fast.

Filling:

2 c. powdered sugar
2 egg whites, beaten

1½ c. Crisco
1 t. vanilla

Mrs. Andy (Lizzie) Miller

tips and hints

PUT SMALL POTATOES IN WASHING MACHINE TO WASH, AND CAN LIKE OTHER VEGETABLES. WHEN YOU OPEN THEM, SLICE POTATOES AND SAUSAGE AND FRY, THEN POUR EGGS OVER THEM. A SIMPLE, GOOD MEAL.

MRS. DAN (MARY) MILLER

LITTLE DEBBIE COOKIES

3 c. flour	2$^1/_4$ t. soda
1$^1/_2$ t. salt	2 T. boiling water
$^3/_4$ t. nutmeg	3 t. cinnamon
2$^1/_4$ c. oleo	1 T. vanilla
6 eggs	4$^1/_2$ c. brown sugar
3 c. raisins or nuts, optional	6 c. quick oatmeal

Cream sugar, oleo and eggs. Add vanilla and soda, which has been dissolved in boiling water. Then add the rest of ingredients and mix well. Drop by spoonsful on cookie sheets and bake at 350°. Frost with filling and sandwich cookies.

Filling:

3 egg whites, beaten	$^1/_4$ c. Crisco
1 t. vanilla	3 c. powdered sugar

We were expecting many relatives from other communities for Jacob and Mable's wedding, so I decided to bake Little Debbie cookies for our visitors. The next day neighbors came to help get ready for the wedding. When they wanted to put something in the oven, they found a pan with some black lumps on it. Yesterday's forgotten cookies, burned to a crisp!

Mrs. Harvey L. (Martha) Mast

The hearts that love will never know winter's frost and chill; summer's warmth is in them still.

Wooden Spoon Wedding Cookbook   **155**

WHOOPIE PIE COOKIES

4 c. flour	1 c. cocoa
2 c. sugar	2 eggs
2 t. soda	2 t. vanilla
1 t. salt	1^1/$_4$ c. sour milk
1 c. shortening	1^1/$_4$ c. cold water

Cream together sugar, salt, shortening, vanilla and eggs. Sift together flour, soda and cocoa. Add this to the first mixture alternately with water and sour milk. Add slightly more flour if milk is not thick. Drop by teaspoonsful on greased cookie sheet. Bake at 400°. Yield: approximately 50 cookies.

Filling:

1 (8 oz.) pkg. cream cheese	^{1}/$_2$ t. vanilla
^{1}/$_2$ c. butter, softened	7-8 c. confectioner's sugar

Cream together cream cheese, butter and vanilla. Add confectioner's sugar. Spread between two cookies.

Mrs. Ervin (Mary) Byler

CAKE MIX COOKIES

^{1}/$_2$ c. white sugar	1 pkg. instant pudding
1^1/$_2$ c. brown sugar	1 cake mix
2 c. oleo	2 t. baking soda
6 eggs	5 c. all-purpose flour

Mix in order given. Drop on cookie sheets and flatten with a glass dipped in white sugar. Make sandwich cookies with whoopie pie filling. Bake at 350°. If you want chocolate cookies, use a chocolate cake mix and pudding. Or you can use a yellow cake mix and vanilla pudding.

Mrs. Levi (Mary) Miller, Mrs. Jonas D.A. (Edna) Miller

ABE MARY COOKIES

5 c. brown sugar	3 T. baking powder
1¹/₂ c. buttermilk	6 eggs
1¹/₂ c. sweet milk	2 T. vanilla
3 c. butter and lard	1 t. salt
2 T. soda	flour till right (5 lbs.)

Mix sugar, butter and lard. Add buttermilk and some flour—add eggs and
stir well. Add rest of ingredients and mix well. For variation add several
cups of chocolate chips.

Frosting:

¹/₂ c. butter, slightly browned	1 t. maple flavoring
1 c. brown sugar	¹/₂ t. salt
¹/₄ c. milk	powdered sugar

Slightly brown butter and add brown sugar. Keep stirring for 1 minute.
Add milk and cook. Take off heat and add maple flavoring and salt.
Add powdered sugar until the right consistency. Don't make too thick
with powdered sugar, as it thickens as it cools. I got this recipe from my
mother's uncle's wife (Abe Mary).

Mrs. John D. (Katie) Miller

MAPLE LEAF COOKIES

1 lb. butter	1 t. salt
4 c. brown sugar	12 T. cream
8 eggs	10$^{1}/_{2}$ c. flour
2 T. soda	4 T. maple flavoring

Cream butter and sugar. Add remaining ingredients in order given. Do not overbake. Use maple leaf design cookie cutter. Bake at 350°-375°.

Frosting:

2 egg whites, beaten	2 T. flour
1 T. vanilla	2 c. powdered sugar
1 t. cream of tartar	

Mix together and beat well. Add $^{1}/_{2}$ c. Crisco and $^{3}/_{4}$ c. marshmallow topping. Cream until smooth.

Mrs. Jacob (Esther) Miller

PIE CRUST COOKIES

16 c. flour	4 t. soda
4 c. shortening	8 eggs
8 c. brown sugar	milk
4 t. vanilla	2 c. chocolate chips
8 t. baking powder	

Mix dry ingredients as for pie crusts. Beat eggs in 2 qt. pitcher, then fill with milk and add. Add vanilla and chocolate chips. Bake at 350°.

Martha Miller

PIE CRUST COOKIES

1 c. white sugar	4 c. flour
1 c. brown sugar	1 c. lard
1/2 t. salt	2 eggs
1 t. soda	milk
2 t. baking powder	1 t. vanilla

Mix dry ingredients. Cut in lard until mixture resembles coarse crumbs. Break eggs into 1 c. measuring cup. Beat, then fill cup with milk. Stir in vanilla. Combine liquid with dry ingredients. Drop by teaspoonsful onto greased cookie sheet. Bake at 350° for 12 minutes.

MONSTER COOKIES

1 c. brown sugar, packed	3/4 t. corn syrup
1 c. white sugar	4 1/2 c. quick oatmeal
3 eggs	2 t. soda
1/2 c. oleo	1/2 c. M&Ms
1 1/2 c. peanut butter	1/2 c. chocolate chips
3/4 t. vanilla	

Mix all together and drop by tablespoons onto cookie sheet. Bake for 10-12 minutes at 350°.

Mrs. Eli (Ella) Stutzman

CAKES, COOKIES & FROSTINGS

CHOCOLATE PINWHEELS

1 c. butter
2 c. sugar
$^1/_2$ c. brown sugar
2 eggs
1 T. vanilla

$3^3/_4$ c. flour
2 t. baking powder
pinch of salt
$^1/_4$ c. cocoa

Mix dough and divide in half to separate bowls; add cocoa to 1 bowl. Roll out each portion between waxed paper into a 10" x 12" rectangle. Refrigerate 30 minutes. Put plain dough on top of chocolate and roll up tightly, jelly roll style. Refrigerate 2 hours, then slice and bake.

Mrs. John (Susan) Miller

CRISPY CEREAL MERINGUES

4 egg whites
$^1/_4$ t. cream of tartar
$^1/_4$ t. salt
1 c. sugar

2 c. chocolate flavored crisp
   rice cereal
$^1/_4$ c. chocolate chips
$^1/_2$ t. butter

Beat egg whites, cream of tartar and salt until soft peaks form. Gradually add sugar 1 tablespoon at a time, until stiff peaks form. Fold in cereal. Drop by rounded teaspoonful. Bake at 300° for 35-40 minutes or until firm to touch. Melt chocolate chips and butter. Put in a Zip-Lock bag; cut a small hole in corner of bag. Drizzle melted chocolate over cookies. Place on wax paper to harden.

160   *Wooden Spoon Wedding Cookbook*

CAKES, COOKIES & FROSTINGS

MULE EARS

3 c. brown sugar
1¹/₂ c. shortening
3 eggs
1¹/₄ c. dark Karo, scant

2 t. ginger
1 T. soda
2 t. cinnamon
7 c. flour

Add flour until dough is right consistency. Shape into rolls and chill. Slice.
Bake at 350° for 10-15 minutes or until lightly browned.

Mrs. Dan (Emma) Miller

CHOCOLATE FROSTING

1 c. cold milk
1 box chocolate instant pudding

8 oz. Ready Whip

Beat milk and pudding until thick. Add Ready Whip. Spread over cake. A
very fluffy frosting!

BUTTERCREAM FROSTING

¹/₂ c. solid vegetable shortening
¹/₂ c. butter
1 t. vanilla

4 c. sifted powdered sugar
2 T. milk

Cream butter and shortening. Add vanilla. Gradually add sugar, one cup at
a time, beating well after each addition. Scrape sides and bottom of bowl
often. When all sugar has been mixed in, icing will appear dry. Add milk
and beat until light and fluffy. For medium consistency icing, add 1¹/₂-2 T.
light corn syrup. For thin consistency, add 3-4 T. light corn syrup. Thick
consistency is used to make flowers, medium for other decorations and
thin to frost the cake.

Wooden Spoon Wedding Cookbook   161

BROWN SUGAR FROSTING

½ c. butter   1 c. brown sugar
1 c. milk   powdered sugar

Melt butter; add milk and brown sugar. Boil a few minutes, stirring often. Cool completely. Add enough powdered sugar for the right consistency.

Every Amish girl receives a china set from her parents. I got to choose my set and this is what I chose. It is called "Blue Rose," as the roses are a pretty blue. This china set was used at our wedding in the "eck." Now it is displayed in my china hutch, almost too pretty to use.

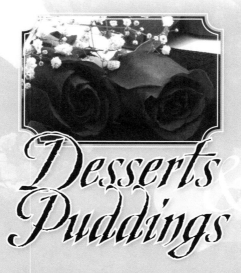

Desserts & Puddings

To choose a pudding, it was not hard;
In weddings date pudding seems to be a part.
The dessert that is so creamy and sweet,
Layered high in a bowl, oh so neat!

There's many different recipes out there,
But not as good as my mom's, I declare!
Dates, bananas and a butterscotch filling,
To taste it there are few who are not willing.

My cousins had the job of fixing it;
They sure didn't have much time to sit.
Beat the topping and the bananas slice,
Take time to layer it real nice!

Many bowls were fixed and in the ice-house set;
Not much was left when everyone was fed.
And so that's proof enough that it was good.
Try making your own, I really think you could.

*W*e had 432 ice cream cups delivered on our wedding day. We had 150 left, so we put them in the neighbors' freezers and enjoyed them later. Soon after we moved, my whole family came to help us rake and mow our lawn. They brought some of the ice cream along for a snack. So we had a double treat that evening. Help in the yard and ice cream!

Aden and Miriam
October 2, 2003

Date Pudding

2 c. dates
2 t. soda
2 c. white sugar
2 T. butter
2 c. boiling water
2 c. flour
2 eggs
½ c. nuts

Mix dates, soda and sugar. Pour boiling water over it; add butter. Let set until cool. Add flour, eggs and nuts. Bake in two 13" x 9" x 2" pans at 400°. When cold, cut or break into small pieces and fill serving bowl alternately with layers of cake pieces, bananas, instant butterscotch pudding (mixed as directed) and sweetened whipped cream.

The Saturday before the wedding, Mom (with Sarah's help) made 12 batches of this cake. It was cut and stored in bowls. October 2nd came and 6 girls could be found beating, slicing and layering till they had plenty of bowls filled for everyone to get their share.

Aden and Miriam
October 2, 2003

Crust Salad

2 c. flour
½ c. brown sugar
½ c. chopped nuts
¾ c. margarine
1 (15 oz.) can crushed pineapple

¾ c. orange Jell-O
8 oz. cream cheese
¾ c. white sugar
2 c. unwhipped Rich's topping

Mix flour, sugar, nuts and margarine with wire whisk. Press into greased 13" x 9" pan. Bake at 375° for 15 minutes. Heat pineapple (undrained) to boiling. Add Jell-O. Stir to dissolve. Cool. Beat sugar and cream cheese. Fold into Jell-O mixture. Whip Rich's topping and fold into Jell-O mixture. Pour on crust. Refrigerate.

On Friday before the wedding the crust was baked. We baked 12 batches and let them cool, then pressed the crust in Rubbermaid pans that came with the wedding dishes. The day before the wedding, my aunts made the top layer and poured it over the crusts. Then they were stored in the icehouse all ready for supper the next day.

Aden and Miriam
October 2, 2003

Danish Dessert
(for mixed fruit)

1 1/3 c. white sugar
1/3 c. Perma-Flo

1/2 c. orange Jell-O
1/2 c. pineapple Jell-O

Mix dry ingredients. Add 8 c. fruit juice and water. Bring to a boil. Remove from heat. Cool.

We made 6 batches of this Danish Dessert, and I filled 3 ice cream pails. The day of the wedding 5 girls chunked apples and peaches, cut red and green grapes in half and added pineapple chunks. They had enough fruit to fill three 13 qt. mixing bowls plus a Fix-n-Mix. They poured the Danish over the fruit, mixed it, put it in serving bowls and set it on the table.

DESSERTS & PUDDINGS

Wedding Date Pudding and Sauce

1. chopped dates	1 c. brown sugar
1 c. boiling water	1 c. Thesco flour
1 T. butter	1 t. vanilla
1 egg, beaten	1/4 c. nuts, optional

Pour boiling water over dates and butter. Cool; add rest of ingredients. Use large foil pans. Make a double batch for one pan. Cut, 24 blocks to 1 pan.

Date Pudding Sauce:

1/2 c. butter, browned	1 1/2 c. water
3 c. brown sugar	3/4 c. clear jel
3 c. water	1 t. vanilla
1/4 t. salt	1/2 t. maple flavoring

Boil first four ingredients together a few minutes. Mix last four ingredients and add to boiling part. Use 1/4 c. sauce for each block of date pudding. Use one batch sauce for one large foil pan. Sprinkle crushed Heath bars on top.

Mrs. Uriah (Sevilla) Yoder

DESSERTS & PUDDINGS

Cracker-Cream Cheese Pudding

9 c. milk
1¹/₂ c. white sugar
1¹/₂ c. brown sugar
1¹/₂ c. cornstarch
1¹/₂ t. salt

3 T. butter
1 T. vanilla
6 egg yolks
3 c. milk
1 (8 oz.) pkg. cream cheese

Heat 9 c. milk. Make thickening with dry ingredients and 3 c. milk. Pour into hot milk and stir until thickened. Beat egg yolks. Beat ¹/₂-1 c. hot mixture into yolks, then pour into hot mixture and bring just to boil, so it won't get thin after eggs are added. Remove from heat; add cream cheese, butter and vanilla. Stir until melted. Cool. Fix in layers with crackers.

Cracker Crumbs:
3³/₄ c. crushed graham crackers
²/₃ c. brown sugar

1 c. butter

Mix and brown a little

Nine batches of this pudding was made and served at our wedding in 1997.

Mrs. Atlee V. (Barbara) Wengerd

DATE PUDDING

2 c. dates
2¹/₂ t. soda
2 T. butter
2 c. boiling water
1 c. brown sugar

2 eggs
2 t. vanilla
¹/₂ t. salt
3 c. flour

Butterscotch Sauce:
¹/₂ c. butter
1 c. brown sugar
2 c. water

clear jel
1 t. salt
1 t. vanilla

Pour boiling water over first 3 ingredients. Cool; add rest of ingredients. Bake at 350°. For sauce, melt butter, then add sugar. Brown a little, then add water. Bring to a boil; thicken with several tablespoons clear jel. Add salt and vanilla. Arrange in layers with whipped topping. Use chocolate ice cream topping to make a design on top. One batch fills approximately three medium bowls. This recipe will not get soggy as quick.

Mrs. John D. (Katie) Miller

tips and hints

A SUBSTITUTE FOR UNSWEETENED CHOCOLATE: USE 1
T. SHORTENING PLUS 3 T. OF UNSWEETENED COCOA TO
EQUAL 1 SQUARE (1 OZ.) OF UNSWEETENED CHOCOLATE.

OREO COOKIE PUDDING

15 oz. Oreo cookies
8 oz. cream cheese
1 (3 oz.) instant chocolate pudding

1 (3 oz.) instant vanilla pudding
1 large container Cool Whip

Mix chocolate pudding with 2 c. milk. Do this first so pudding will be firm enough to spread. First layer: Smash the Oreos into little bits. Save some for top. Put the rest in the bottom of pan. Second layer: Mix Cool Whip, vanilla pudding and cream cheese together. Spread half of this mixture on top of first layer. Third layer: Add chocolate pudding mixture. Fourth layer: Add rest of Cool Whip mixture. Fifth layer: Sprinkle the rest of crumbs on top. Refrigerate several hours. Can be made a day ahead.

The layer of chocolate seems to make this pudding special. Before we got married Aden thought our Oreo pudding is better than what his sisters made. He tried to convince them to use our recipe, but his sisters claimed the only reason he likes it better is because I made it. They must have changed their mind at some point, as they now also use this recipe.

FLORIDA PUDDING

1 c. flour
$^{1}/_{2}$ c. oleo
$^{1}/_{2}$ c. nuts
8 oz. cream cheese
$1^{1}/_{2}$ c. powdered sugar

$1^{1}/_{2}$ c. whipped cream
1 box vanilla instant pudding
1 box butterscotch pudding
$3^{1}/_{2}$ c. milk

For first layer mix flour, oleo and nuts together. Press into 9" x 13" pan. Bake 5 minutes at 350°. Cool. For second layer mix cream cheese, powdered sugar and whipped cream and spread on cooled crust. For third layer mix vanilla and butterscotch puddings and milk together. Top with whipped cream if desired.

Verba Miller

DESSERTS & PUDDINGS

ANGEL FOOD CAKE PUDDING

1 angel food cake
4 egg yolks
2 c. powdered sugar
crushed

$^1/_2$ c. butter, softened
2 c. whipped topping
3 Butterfinger candy bars,

Cut angel food cake into small pieces. Beat egg yolks, sugar and butter; add topping and $^1/_2$ of the crushed candy bars. Put in layers in a large serving bowl. Garnish with the rest of candy bars.

LAYERED TOFFEE CAKE

2 c. whipping cream
$^1/_2$ c. caramel or butterscotch
    ice cream topping
$^1/_2$ t. vanilla

1 (16 oz.) angel food cake
9 (1.4 oz.) Heath candy bars,
    chopped

Beat cream just until it begins to thicken. Gradually add the ice cream topping and vanilla, beating until soft peaks form. Cut cake horizontally into three layers. Place bottom layer on serving plate; spread with 1 c. cream mixture and sprinkle with $^1/_2$ c. candy bars. Repeat. Place top layer on cake; frost top and sides with remaining cream mixture and sprinkle with remaining candy bars.

tips and hints

ADD A TEASPOON OF VINEGAR TO COOKED ICING. THIS

WILL KEEP IT FROM CRACKING WHEN IT IS CUT.

MRS. DAN (EMMA) MILLER

DESSERTS & PUDDINGS

CHOCOLATE TRIFLE

1 chocolate cake	$^1/_2$ c. strong coffee
1 (6 oz.) pkg. chocolate instant pudding	12 oz. whipped topping
	6 (1.4 oz.) Heath bars, crushed

Bake a cake mix or one from scratch. Cool. Prepare pudding according to directions; set aside. Crumble cake; reserve $^1/_2$ cup. Place half of the remaining cake crumbs in the bottom of a glass bowl. Layer with half of coffee, half of pudding, half of topping and half of candy bars. Repeat layers. Combine remaining crushed candy bars and crumbled cake. Sprinkle over top. Refrigerate 4 to 5 hours.

My parents have a goat and more milk than they can use, so they keep us in milk also. When I asked Mom what they want for the milk she said, "Ask Dad." Dad's answer: "A pan of pudding." When I saw this chocolate trifle recipe I knew that's what I'll take, as Dad loves to sample new recipes. It was a big hit and my youngest brother didn't want to eat anything except pudding. ☺

GRAHAM CRACKER CRUST

1$^1/_4$ c. graham cracker crumbs (approximately 20 squares)	3 T. butter, melted
3 T. sugar	1 egg white

Mix cracker crumbs, sugar and butter. Add egg white, stir until moistened. Press mixture onto the bottom and up the sides of a 9" pie pan. Bake at 375° for 8-10 minutes or until lightly browned. Cool completely before filling.

Mrs. John D. (Katie) Miller

A friend is a person with whom I may be sincere. Before him I may think aloud.

Wooden Spoon Wedding Cookbook   173

CREAM CHEESE CRACKER PUDDING

3 c. milk
1 c. sugar
$^1/_2$ c. cornstarch
$^1/_2$ t. salt
2 eggs

1 t. vanilla
1 T. butter
1 c. milk
4 oz. cream cheese

Heat 3 c. milk. Mix dry ingredients with eggs and 1 c. milk. Add to hot milk and stir until boiling. Add butter, vanilla and cream cheese. Stir until cheese is melted. Very good to put in layers with crushed graham crackers, or use it for Oreo pudding.

Mrs. Levi (Mary) Miller

GRAHAM CRACKER PUDDING

2 pkg. graham crackers, crushed
4 T. brown sugar
$^1/_2$ c. butter, browned
10 c. milk
$1^1/_3$ c. cornstarch
$^1/_2$ c. flour

$^2/_3$ c. white sugar
2 c. milk
8 egg yolks
$2^1/_4$ c. brown sugar
4 T. butter
2 t. vanilla

Mix 4 T. brown sugar and butter with crackers. To make the pudding, heat 10 c. milk. Stir together the next 5 ingredients. Put it in the heated milk and boil again. Then add the last 3 ingredients. Stir once in awhile while cooling to keep it smooth. Add whipped topping before putting in layers.

Mrs. Andy (Lizzie) Miller

GRAHAM CRACKER PUDDING

2¹/₂ c. graham crackers, crushed
²/₃ c. melted butter
¹/₄ c. white sugar

1 c. powdered sugar
8 oz. cream cheese
1 c. whipped topping

Mix crackers, butter and sugar. Toast at 350° for 8-10 minutes. For second layer beat cream cheese; add powdered sugar. Whip topping and add to cream cheese mixture, a little at a time so it doesn't get lumpy. Top with your favorite thickened fruit.

HOT FUDGE PUDDING

2 T. butter
1 T. cocoa
1²/₃ c. water

³/₄ c. white sugar
¹/₂ t. salt

Dough:
1 c. sifted flour
¹/₂ c. milk
1 t. baking powder
1 T. cocoa

³/₄ c. sugar
¹/₂ c. chopped nuts
2 T. butter

Put all together in saucepan and boil 5 minutes. Pour into baking pan. Mix dough ingredients and pour over syrup mixture. Bake at 350° for 45 minutes. Serve warm with ice cream or whipped cream.

Rebecca Yoder, Martha Miller

BUTTERSCOTCH TAPIOCA

6 c. boiling water
1 t. salt
1¹/₂ c. tapioca
2 c. brown sugar
2 eggs, beaten
¹/₂ c. white sugar

1 c. milk
¹/₂ c. butter, browned
2 t. vanilla
whipped cream
bananas and Milky Way candy
bars, optional

Cook boiling water, salt and tapioca for 15 minutes. Add brown sugar and cook until tapioca is done. Stir often. Mix beaten eggs, sugar and milk and add to tapioca mixture. Cook until it bubbles. Then stir in browned butter and vanilla. Add whipped cream, bananas and Milky Way candy bars.

Mrs. Mahlon (Katie) Miller

PEARL TAPIOCA WITH CREAM CHEESE

6 c. boiling water
1 c. pearl tapioca
1 T. salt
1 c. white sugar
¹/₄ c. strawberry Jell-O

1 (8 oz.) pkg. cream cheese
2 c. cream or ¹/₂ can Rich's
topping
1 can crushed pineapples, optional

Bring water to a rolling boil. Add tapioca. Keep at a rolling boil (keeping covered) for 5-10 minutes. Stir a few times while boiling. Remove from heat. Add sugar, salt and Jell-O immediately. Stir until dissolved. Cover immediately and set aside to cool. Stir once it is cold. Before serving, beat cream, add cream cheese and mix into tapioca. Serves 12 people.

Mrs. Atlee V. (Barbara) Wengerd

DESSERTS & PUDDINGS

PINEAPPLE FLUFF

1 lb. marshmallows	1¹/₂ pkg. graham crackers, crushed
1 c. pineapple juice	¹/₂ c. butter, melted
2³/₄ c. Rich's topping, before whipped	

Heat marshmallows and juice in top of double boiler, just until marshmallows are melted. Let cool but not until stiff. Add the topping and mix well. Mix crackers and melted butter. Put in layers—crackers then pudding then crackers.

Mrs. David D. (Emma) Miller

PINEAPPLE PRETZEL FLUFF

1 c. coarsely crushed pretzels	20 oz. crushed pineapple, drained
¹/₂ c. butter, melted	12 oz. frozen whipped topping,
1 c. sugar, divided	thawed
8 oz. cream cheese, softened	

Combine pretzels, butter and ¹/₂ c. sugar. Bake at 400° for 7 minutes. Cool. Meanwhile, beat cream cheese and remaining sugar until creamy. Fold in pineapple and whipped topping. Chill until serving. Break pretzel mixture into small pieces. Stir into pineapple mixture. Serves 6 people.

MALLOW CREAM

2 c. miniature marshmallows	1 t. lemon juice
1 c. crushed pineapple	¹/₄ c. whipping cream, whipped

In a saucepan combine marshmallows, pineapple and lemon juice. Cook and stir over low heat until marshmallows are melted and mixture is blended. Cover and chill until mixture is partially set. Fold in whipped cream. Cover and chill for at least 30 minutes.

If we love people, we will see them as God intends them to be.

Wooden Spoon Wedding Cookbook

DESSERTS & PUDDINGS

HOMEMADE ICE CREAM

2 pkg. unflavored gelatin
³/₄ c. cold water
1 pt. milk
2 T. cornstarch
1 c. white sugar

6 eggs, separated
1 t. vanilla
1 t. salt
2 c. brown sugar
1 can Eagle Brand milk

Soak gelatin in cold water and set aside. Cook together milk and cornstarch. While still hot add white sugar, beaten egg yolks and gelatin mixture. Later, when cooled, add vanilla, salt, brown sugar and Eagle Brand milk. Add beaten egg whites. Put in 1¹/₂ gal. can and fill can with milk. Can also add any flavor instant pudding if desired.

Mrs. Jacob (Esther) Miller

FRUIT SALAD

8 oz. cream cheese
8 oz. Ready Whip

1 can sweetened condensed milk

Mix together and add grapes, apples, strawberries, raspberries, pineapples, bananas or just any fruit you like.

Mrs. Ivan (Mary) Miller

TROPICAL FRUIT DESSERT

1¹/₄ c. sugar
¹/₂ c. clear jel
4 c. water
2 T. tropical drink mix

6 bananas
1 can chunk pineapples
1 c. red seedless grapes

In a medium saucepan combine sugar, clear jel and drink mix. Stir in water. Bring to a boil over medium heat. Cool; chill in refrigerator, then add fruit.

Mrs. John (Fannie) Miller

178 *Wooden Spoon Wedding Cookbook*

These napkins were square when we got them, but I made a pattern and folded each one. My great-aunt who is almost blind, folded some of them for me as a pastime, since she can't see to work or even read. This was something she could feel to do, instead of seeing.

DESSERTS & PUDDINGS

SLUSH

1 (12 oz.) frozen orange juice
2 c. white sugar
4 c. cold water
1 can crushed pineapple and juice

1 can chunk pineapple and juice
6 bananas, sliced
1 can mandarin oranges and juice
1 bunch grapes

Mix and freeze. Can also be frozen in the ice cream freezer like ice cream.
Great on a warm summer day!

Miriam Miller

COOKED APPLE SNITZ

6 c. water
1 1/2 c. brown sugar
1 1/2 c. white sugar
1 T. vinegar

8 T. Perma-Flo
pinch of salt
12 apples

Bring first 6 ingredients to a boil. When thickened add apples, peeled and
quartered as desired. Bring to a boil again and cook for 2 or 3 minutes.
This is a favorite with our Christmas brunch.

Mrs. Jacob (Esther) Miller

DESSERTS & PUDDINGS

APPLE DUMPLINGS

2 c. flour	2 c. peeled, chopped tart apples
1 t. salt	2 c. packed brown sugar
²/₃ c. shortening	1 c. water
4-5 T. cold water	¹/₄ c. butter, cubed

Combine flour and salt; cut in shortening until crumbly. Gradually add water, tossing with a fork until dough forms a ball. On a lightly floured surface, roll out dough to a 12" x 18" rectangle. Cut into 6 squares. Place ¹/₃ c. chopped apples in the center of each square. Brush edges of dough with water; fold up corners to center and pinch to seal. Place on a greased 9" x 13" pan. Bake at 350° for 30 minutes. In a saucepan combine brown sugar, water and butter; bring to a boil, stirring constantly. Pour over dumplings. Bake 25-30 minutes longer or until apples are tender.

We have our own apple trees, but the apples are small and most of them have spots that need to be cut out, so I like to use this recipe instead of one that uses a half apple for each dumpling.

RED AND GREEN GELATIN

1 (3 oz.) pkg. lime gelatin	2 c. large marshmallows
2 c. boiling water, divided	1 (3 oz.) pkg. cherry gelatin
1 (8 oz.) can crushed pineapple, undrained	1 c. cherry pie filling

In a small bowl, dissolve lime gelatin in 1 c. boiling water. Let stand 2 minutes. Stir in pineapple. Pour into an 11" x 7" x 2" pan. Top with marshmallows. Cover and refrigerate until set. Dissolve cherry gelatin in remaining boiling water. Let stand for 2 minutes. Stir in pie filling; pour over marshmallows. Cover and refrigerate until set. Serves 12 people.

Life has no blessings like a faithful friend.

Wooden Spoon Wedding Cookbook

DESSERTS & PUDDINGS

LIME DELIGHT

1 (8 oz.) can crushed pineapples,
   undrained
¹/₄ c. lime gelatin (powder)

¹/₂ c. cream-style cottage cheese
1 c. whipped topping

In a small saucepan, bring pineapples to a boil over medium heat. Remove from heat. Stir in gelatin until dissolved. Chill until slightly thickened (approximately 30 minutes). Stir in the cottage cheese and whipped topping. Refrigerate.

Mrs. Ivan A. Miller

LIME SALAD (SUGAR-FREE)

2 c. flour
¹/₂ c. nuts, if desired
¹/₂ c. butter
1 (20 oz.) can crushed pineapple

3 oz. lime Jell-O (sugar-free)
1¹/₂ c. Rich's topping
8 oz. cream cheese

Mix flour, nuts and butter; press into 13" x 9" x 2" pan. Bake at 350° for 15 minutes. Cool. Bring undrained pineapples to a boil. Add Jell-O; cool. Whip Rich's topping. Cream the cream cheese and whipped topping together. Add to cooled Jell-O-pineapple mixture. Pour onto cooled crust. Refrigerate.

Mrs. John (Katie) Troyer

182   *Wooden Spoon Wedding Cookbook*

RIBBON SALAD

3 oz. green Jell-O
2 c. miniature marshmallows
1 small can pineapple
3 oz. red Jell-O

8 oz. cream cheese
3 oz. lemon Jell-O
1 c. whipped topping

First layer: Mix green Jell-O as directed. Second layer: Melt the marshmallows in the lemon Jell-O; add pineapple, cream cheese and whipped topping. Third layer: Mix red Jell-O as directed.

Mrs. Eli (Ella) Stutzman

CHERRY GELATIN SALAD

8 oz. unsweetened crushed
   pineapple, undrained
$^1/_2$ c. water
1 (3 oz.) pkg. sugar-free
   cherry gelatin

1 (3 oz.) pkg. sugar-free
   lemon gelatin
1 (12 oz.) can diet cola
15 oz. pitted dark sweet cherries,
   drained and chopped

In a saucepan, bring pineapple and water to a boil. Stir in cherry and lemon gelatin until dissolved. Stir in cola and cherries. Pour into a greased pan. Refrigerate until firm.

DELICIOUS JELL-O MOLD

2 (3 oz.) boxes Jell-O, any flavor
1 can sweetened condensed milk

1 c. hot water
16 oz. Cool Whip

Mix together hot water and Jell-O until dissolved and ready to set. Add milk and mix well. Then add Cool Whip. Mix all together. Pour into Jell-O mold. Garnish if desired.

Mrs. Ivan A. Miller

A successful marriage is one in which you fall in love many times, always with the same person.

Wooden Spoon Wedding Cookbook   **183**

DESSERTS & PUDDINGS

MANDARIN ORANGE SALAD

2 eggs, beaten
1 c. orange juice
$^1/_2$ c. sugar
2 T. flour

1 (10 oz.) pkg. miniature
   marshmallows
1 (8 oz.) pkg. cream cheese
1 can mandarin oranges, drained
1 can crushed pineapples, drained

Combine the first 4 ingredients and juice from oranges and pineapple in a 2 qt. saucepan and cook until thick, stirring constantly. Remove from heat and immediately add marshmallows and cream cheese. Stir until all is melted and smooth. When cold add oranges and pineapple. Fold in 1 c. cream (whipped) or 1 pkg. Dream Whip. Mix and pour in dish.

Elmina Miller

ICE CREAM SALAD

$^1/_3$ c. Jell-O
1 c. hot water

1 pt. ice cream

If ice cream is melted, cool Jell-O a little before adding ice cream. Add fruit if desired.

Martha Miller

tips and hints

TO CLEAN DIRTY FAUCETS, TIE A RAG AROUND THE

FAUCET, THEN SOAK THE RAG WITH VINEGAR AND

LEAVE ON FOR A FEW HOURS. REMOVE RAG AND STAINS

SHOULD BE GONE.

MRS. DAN (MARY) MILLER

184   *Wooden Spoon Wedding Cookbook*

The bridal party ate supper with the married people, but saved dessert to eat with the young folks. Aden's brother and his wife fixed the sundaes. A layer of Heath bits, scoops of vanilla ice cream, a layer of Magic Shell ice cream topping and topped with a red cherry. A Twix candy bar stuck in the side put on the finishing touch. A highlight for the nieces and nephews is to bring the sundaes to the bridal party. Each child receives a small gift.

INDIANA SALAD

First Layer:
1 c. any flavor Jell-O
2 c. hot water

3 c. cold water
1 (20 oz.) can crushed pineapple

Second Layer:
8 oz. cream cheese

1^1/$_2$ c. Rich's topping

Third Layer:
2 c. pineapple juice
1^1/$_4$ c. sugar
4 egg yolks

3 T. clear jel
pinch of salt

Mrs. Alvin (Ida) Miller

FRUIT COBBLER

1 qt. fresh fruit, rhubarb, cherries
   or peaches
3 c. sugar, divided
2 c. flour

1 T. baking powder
2 t. salt
1^1/$_2$ c. milk

Mix fruit and 1 c. sugar; let stand. Melt ^{1}/$_2$ c. oleo in a cake pan. Mix flour, 2 c. sugar, baking powder, salt and milk. Pour fresh fruit over melted oleo. Pour batter over all. Do not mix. Bake at 375° for 45 minutes. Serve warm with milk or ice cream.

BLUEBERRY BUCKLE

$^1/_4$ c. butter	2 c. cake flour
$^3/_4$ c. sugar	2 t. baking powder
1 egg	pinch of salt
$^1/_2$ c. milk	2 c. blueberries

Topping:

$^1/_3$ c. flour	1 t. cinnamon
$^2/_3$ c. sugar	3 T. butter, melted

Mix batter together; add blueberries last. Pour into 9" x 13" pan and top with topping. Pan will be full. Bake at 350°. Serve warm with milk or ice cream.

Mrs. John (Susan) Miller

tips and hints

WITHOUT FRIENDS, LIFE WOULD BE LIKE A GARDEN

WITHOUT FLOWERS.

MRS. HENRY (ALMA) MAST

RHUBARB TORTE

Crust:

1 c. flour

2 T. sugar

dash of salt

$^1/_2$ c. butter

Press into 8" x 10" pan. Bake at 325°.

Filling:

2$^1/_2$ c. chopped rhubarb

1$^1/_4$ c. white sugar

$^1/_2$ c. half & half or milk

2 T. flour

3 egg yolks

Combine in saucepan. Spread over crust.

Topping:

3 egg whites

$^1/_4$ t. cream of tartar

6 T. sugar

Beat egg whites and cream of tartar together. Add sugar gradually until stiff. Spread over rhubarb filling and bake until lightly browned.

Mrs. Jacob D. (Esther) Miller

DESSERTS & PUDDINGS

APPLE CRISP

³/₄ c. sugar   ¹/₂ t. cinnamon
¹/₄ t. salt   4 c. sliced apples
1 T. flour

Topping:
³/₄ c. oatmeal   ¹/₂ c. brown sugar
³/₄ c. flour   ³/₄ c. butter
¹/₄ t. soda   ³/₄ t. baking powder

Mix sugar, flour, salt and cinnamon with apples. Mix well and place in a casserole dish. For topping, combine dry ingredients and rub in butter to make crumbs. Put crumbs on top of apple mixture. Bake at 350° for 45 minutes. Serve hot or cold. Delicious with ice cream. Can also use other fruits.

Barbara Miller

APPLE CRISP

4 c. chopped apples   2 T. flour
³/₄ c. white sugar   2 t. cinnamon

Topping:
1 c. brown sugar   ¹/₂ c. soft oleo
1 c. flour   ¹/₄ t. soda
1 c. oatmeal   ¹/₄ t. baking powder

Mix together and place in a 9" x 13" loaf pan. Mix topping ingredients and place on top of apple mixture. Bake at 350° for 30 minutes or until golden brown. Serve warm with milk or ice cream.

Mrs. Eli (Ella) Stutzman

Love is like a fabric that never fades when washed in the water of adversity and grief.

Wooden Spoon Wedding Cookbook   **189**

DESSERTS & PUDDINGS

CORN PONE

1^1/$_2$ c. fine cornmeal	1 t. soda
1^1/$_2$ c. flour	1 egg
1 c. sugar	^{1}/$_2$ c. oleo
2 t. baking powder	^{1}/$_4$-^{1}/$_2$ c. milk

Mix in order given. Dough will be stiff. Bake at 350° until done. Serve with any fruit and milk.

Mrs. Dan (Emma) Miller

CORN PONE

1^1/$_2$ c. flour	^{3}/$_4$ t. soda
^{3}/$_4$ c. cornmeal	^{1}/$_4$ c. lard, melted
^{3}/$_4$ c. white sugar	1 egg
^{1}/$_2$ t. salt	milk, till desired consistency
^{3}/$_4$ t. baking powder	

Mix all together and pour into 8" cake pan. Bake at 350°. Serve warm with fruit and milk.

Mrs. Jacob (Esther) Miller

BROWN BETTY

2^1/$_2$ c. sliced peaches or any desired fruit	^{1}/$_2$ t. soda
1 c. whole wheat flour	^{1}/$_2$ c. brown sugar
^{1}/$_2$ t. salt	1 c. rolled oats
	^{1}/$_2$ c. shortening, scant

Mix all dry ingredients. Mix in shortening until mixture is crumbly. Spread half of mixture in baking pan. Cover with fruit and put rest of crumbs on top. Bake at 350° until nice and brown. Delicious to eat with milk. We like it best with sliced apples, sprinkled with a little cinnamon.

Mrs. Jacob D. (Esther) Miller

PEACH INTRIGUE

$^1/_2$ c. sour cream	$^1/_4$ t. salt
$^1/_2$ t. soda	1 c. flour
$^1/_2$ c. brown sugar	

Cover bottom of pie pan with slices of peaches. Pour dough on top and bake at 350° for 25 minutes or until done. Serve warm with milk.

Mrs. Jacob (Esther) Miller

BROWN SUGAR DUMPLINGS

1 c. brown sugar	$1^1/_2$ t. baking powder
$^3/_4$ c. milk	1 t. vanilla
2 c. flour	1 c. raisins, optional
1 T. butter	

Syrup:

2 c. brown sugar	1 T. butter
2 c. water	

Mix dumpling ingredients together and drop into boiling syrup. Bake at 350°. Serve warm with milk.

Mrs. Jacob (Esther) Miller

CORNSTARCH PUDDING

3 c. sugar	3 T. flour
3 T. cornstarch	6 eggs

Make a paste with the above ingredients and add to 6 pints hot milk. Spoon over chocolate cake while pudding is warm. Eat as warm as possible. It's also good to sprinkle nutmeg over pudding.

Mrs. Dan J. (Mary) Miller

NOTES

Candies & Snacks

A wedding without candy wouldn't be complete;
Parents might tell you otherwise, if the next day you meet.
As the children think candy is the highlight,
So many kinds to choose from, it's hard to decide!

We had many a different kind,
Suckers and Smarties you would find.
No gum, but many a Warhead,
That is what Mom and my siblings said.

Caramels, Skittles and jaw breakers,
M&M's, gummy bears, now and laters,
A variety of candy bars and lots of Rolo's,
Peach rings and bottle caps, on and on the list goes.

Around 30 pounds is what we had,
And this is what I think is bad.
Aden's brothers went upstairs to get their share,
The drawer was empty; it really wasn't fair.

Butter Mints

3 T. soft butter
1/4 t. salt
2 t. peppermint flavoring
1 lb. powdered sugar

1/4 c. cream
1 t. vanilla
food coloring of
    your choice

Put butter in bowl. Alternate sugar and liquids. Mix well. Use table-spoons to measure and roll in white sugar before pressing into sugared molds of your choice.

For our wedding we made 8 batches, which made between 600 and 700 mints. But the amount depends on your mold size. We had white doves, purple grapes and green leaves. The mints were arranged on trays and passed around instead of having candy baskets.

Leroy & Katie Troyer

PARTY MIX

1 box Corn Chex	5 c. mixed nuts
1 box Rice Chex	1 box Honey Combs
1 box Cheerios	1 pkg. Cheetos or Corn Puffs
2 pkg. Bugles	5 T. Worcestershire sauce
1 pkg. pretzels, twists or sticks,	1$^1/_2$ c. butter, melted
broken into pieces	5 t. Lawry's seasoned salt

Mix first eight ingredients in two 13 qt. mixing bowls or 1 large tub. In a
2 qt. saucepan melt butter. Add seasoned salt and Worcestershire sauce.
Pour over cereal and mix well. Put in uncovered roasters. Heat oven to
250°. Slowly toast for 1 hour or more. Stir every 15 minutes. Cool.

Mrs. Atlee V. (Barbara) Wengerd

CRUNCHY POPCORN

1$^1/_2$ gal. popped corn	$^3/_4$ c. packed brown sugar
$^1/_4$ c. oleo	dash of salt
16 large marshmallows	$^1/_4$ c. crunchy peanut butter

Pop the corn. Combine oleo, marshmallows, brown sugar and salt in a
saucepan and cook over low heat until all dissolved. Add peanut butter,
stir, then pour over corn. Stir until evenly coated. By forgetting to add
peanut butter I found out this recipe works for caramel corn if you don't
add peanut butter.

Verba Miller, Mrs. John (Susan) Miller

CARAMEL CORN — FIT FOR A KING

1 c. butter	$^1/_2$ c. light Karo
1 c . white sugar	1 t. salt
1 c. brown sugar	1 t. vanilla

Pop enough popcorn to fill Tupperware Fix and Mix. Bring the rest of ingredients to a boil. Boil for 5 minutes. Remove from heat; stir in 1 t. soda. Pour popcorn in roaster and stir in caramel sauce. Bake in warm oven, not over 250°, for 1 hour; stir every 15 minutes.

Rebecca E. Coblentz

CARAMEL CORN

3 c. brown sugar	$1^1/_2$ c. butter
$^3/_4$ c. light corn syrup	12 qt. popcorn

Combine sugar, corn syrup and butter. Bring to a boil and pour over popped corn. Heat in oven for 1 hour at 250°. Stir often.

Mrs. Leroy (Katie) Miller

POPCORN CAKE

14 c. popped popcorn	6 oz. chocolate chips
$^1/_2$ c. butter	$^1/_2$ c. peanut butter
10 marshmallows	

In a bowl, combine popcorn and chocolate chips; set aside. In a medium saucepan melt butter. Add peanut butter and marshmallows. Cook on low heat until melted, stirring constantly. Pour over popcorn and chocolate chips; stir to coat. Press mixture firmly into a fluted round magic baking form. Remove from pan and cut into slices to serve.

Candy is a big part of a wedding, especially for the children. My youngest sister and Aden's niece got to pass the baskets filled with candy. They were passed around for dinner and supper. We had around 30 pounds, and with all of Aden's nieces and nephews, besides all the other children, we had to hide some for supper. They knew where the candy drawer was, so it was a help-yourself deal.

HOCKY PUCKS (SUGARLESS)

2¹/₂ c. crushed cornflakes
    or Rice Krispies
¹/₂ c. peanut butter

¹/₄ c. honey
1 t. vanilla

Melt peanut butter and honey in a double boiler. Add vanilla and cereal.
Mix well. Roll into small balls. Place onto wax paper to cool. Can be eaten
like this or can be dipped into melted coating chocolate.

Mrs. Atlee V. (Barbara) Wengerd

DONUT HOLES

1¹/₂ c. flour
¹/₃ c. sugar
2 t. baking powder
¹/₂ t. salt

¹/₂ t. nutmeg
1 egg
¹/₂ c. milk
2 T. melted butter

Mix well. Dip out dough with teaspoon. Form 1" balls. Deep-fry at 375°.
While warm, dip in maple syrup or roll in powdered sugar. Eat while
warm. Yield: approximately 50 balls.

Mrs. Dan J. (Mary) Miller

PULL BUNS

1 T. yeast, dissolved in	$^1/_2$ t. salt
$^1/_4$ c. lukewarm water	3 eggs, well beaten
1 c. scalded milk	$^1/_3$ c. white sugar
$^1/_3$ c. butter	$3^3/_4$ c. flour

Sugar Mixture:

$^3/_4$ c. granulated sugar	1 T. cinnamon
$^1/_2$ c. chopped walnuts	

Add sugar, butter and salt to scalded milk. Cool to lukewarm. Add dissolved yeast, eggs and just enough flour to make a stiff batter. Mix well. Cover and let rise until mixture doubles in size. Knead down and let rise again. Make dough into small balls (about the size of walnuts) and dip into melted butter. Roll each ball in sugar mixture. Pile balls loosely in ungreased angel food cake pan. Let rise again for 30 minutes. Bake at 400° for 10 minutes, then lower oven temperature to 350° and bake about 30 minutes or until brown. Turn pan upside down on plate.

Mrs. Ivan A. Miller

PATTIES

2 c. flour	dash of salt
2 eggs, beaten	1 t. vanilla
1 c. milk	2 t. sugar

Mix batter well. Heat oil to deep-fry temperature. Then use pattie iron and dip into batter mixture. Hold into hot oil until it peels off. Dip front side into sugar when cooled off just a bit.

Mrs. John (Susan) Miller

Happy homes are built with bricks of patience, using love for mortar.

CANDIES & SNACKS

GRANOLA BARS

6 T. butter	¹/₄ c. honey
5+ c. mini marshmallows	¹/₂ c. graham cracker crumbs
3¹/₂ c. Rice Krispies	¹/₂ c. coconut
1¹/₂ c. quick oats	¹/₂ c. chocolate chips

Melt butter and marshmallows; add honey. Pour over dry mixture and mix well. Spread on greased cookie sheet and sprinkle with ¹/₂ c. chocolate chips. Press mixture with potato masher and let cool. Cut into bars.

Mrs. Eli (Ella) Stutzman

GRANOLA BARS

¹/₄ c. butter	7 c. Rice Krispies
¹/₂ c. oil	3 c. oatmeal
1 (16 oz.) bag marshmallows	1 c. graham cracker crumbs
¹/₂ c. honey	1 c. coconut

Heat butter and oil on low heat. Add marshmallows and honey; stir until melted. In a large bowl mix together dry ingredients. Pour marshmallow mixture over this and stir well. Last add 1 c. chocolate chips. Press into greased jelly roll pan and chill before cutting.

Mrs. Levi (Mary) Miller

tips and hints

BEFORE MELTING CHOCOLATE, RUB THE INSIDE OF

THE PAN IT IS TO BE MELTED IN WITH BUTTER. THE

CHOCOLATE WILL NOT STICK TO THE PAN.

EMMA MILLER

200 *Wooden Spoon Wedding Cookbook*

3-LAYER KEEBLER BARS

Club crackers
$^3/_4$ c. white sugar
$^1/_2$ c. brown sugar
$^1/_2$ c. butter
1 c. finely crushed graham crackers

$^1/_4$ c. milk
$^1/_2$ c. chocolate chips
$^1/_2$ c. butterscotch chips
$^1/_2$ c. peanut butter

Line a lightly greased 13" x 9" x 2" pan with whole Club crackers. Boil sugars, butter, graham crackers and milk slowly for 5 minutes. Pour over crackers in pan and immediately top with another layer of Club crackers. Allow to cool. Melt chocolate chips, butterscotch chips and peanut butter in saucepan. Spread over top. Cut into bars when cooled.

Mrs. John (Katie) Troyer

S'MORES BARS

12 graham crackers
12 oz. chocolate chips
6 T. butter, divided

10 oz. miniature marshmallows
13 oz. Cocoa Diamonds cereal

Line a 9" x 13" pan with foil. Grease foil. Place graham crackers in bottom of pan. Melt chocolate chips with 2 T. butter. Stir until smooth. Spread over graham crackers. Melt marshmallows with 4 T. butter. When melted add cereal and pour over chocolate. Cool; cut into bars.

Everyone has a gift for something, even if it is the gift of being a good friend.

Wooden Spoon Wedding Cookbook 201

CANDIES & SNACKS

NO-BAKE BARS

4 c. Cheerios
2 c. Crisp Rice cereal
2 c. dry roasted peanuts
2 c. M&Ms

1 c. light corn syrup
1 c. sugar
1¹/₂ c. creamy peanut butter
1 t. vanilla

Combine first 4 ingredients; set aside. In a saucepan, bring corn syrup and sugar to a boil, stirring frequently. Remove from heat; stir in peanut butter and vanilla. Pour over cereal mixture and toss to coat evenly. Spread in a greased 15" x 10" pan. Cool; cut into bars.

CRISPY PRETZEL BARS

1 c. sugar
1 c. light corn syrup
¹/₂ c. peanut butter

5 c. Crisp Rice cereal
2 c. pretzel sticks
1 c. plain M&Ms

In a saucepan combine sugar and corn syrup; stir over low heat until sugar is melted. Stir in peanut butter. Add cereal, pretzels and M&Ms until coated. Press into greased 15" x 10" pan. Cut into bars.

tips and hints

PEANUTS ARE ONE OF THE INGREDIENTS IN

DYNAMITE.

202   *Wooden Spoon Wedding Cookbook*

HOT MUSTARD PRETZEL DIP

¹/₄ c. ground mustard
¹/₄ c. vinegar
¹/₄ c. sugar

1 egg yolk
2 T. honey

Combine mustard and vinegar; let stand for 30 minutes. Whisk in sugar and egg yolk until smooth. Cook over medium heat, whisking constantly, until mixture just begins to simmer and is thickened. Remove from heat; whisk in honey. Chill. Serve with pretzels. This recipe is true to its name: hot. I was surprised with how hot it is with only mustard and vinegar to give it zip.

CREAMY CHEESE BALL

3 (8 oz.) pkg. cream cheese
16 oz. Velveeta cheese
1 T. Worcestershire sauce
1 c. shredded cheddar cheese

1 t. salt
¹/₂ t. seasoning salt
2 t. chopped onion

Cream softened cream cheese and Velveeta together. Add remaining ingredients and mix well. Chill. Serve with crackers.

Elmina Miller

CHRISTMAS WREATH

60 marshmallows
1 c. butter
2 t. vanilla

4 t. green food coloring
7 c. cornflakes
cinnamon red hots

Arrange as a wreath, around a candle. Decorate with cinnamon red hots.

Love makes everything lovely; hate concentrates itself on the one hated.

Wooden Spoon Wedding Cookbook   203

CHOCOLATE PEANUT BUTTER PEBBLES

12 oz. chocolate chips
1 c. crunchy peanut butter

4 c. mini marshmallows

Melt chocolate chips and peanut butter. Stir together until blended. Cool 5 minutes. Add marshmallows and stir until blended. Drop by teaspoonsful onto wax paper. Refrigerate until firm.

CHOCOLATE-COVERED SNACK MIX

8 c. Crispix cereal
4 c. Cheerios
3 c. stick pretzels
2 c. dry roasted peanuts

$^1/_2$ lb. plain M&M candies
$^1/_2$ lb. peanut M&M candies
1 lb. white chocolate

Combine cereals, pretzels, peanuts and M&Ms in a very large mixing bowl. Melt chocolate in a double boiler or very slowly in the microwave. Pour melted chocolate over dry mix and stir gently to coat. Stir every 15 minutes until chocolate is dry.

Rebecca E. Coblentz

STRAWBERRY MARSHMALLOW SQUARES

$^1/_4$ c. butter
40 marshmallows

$^1/_3$ c. strawberry Jell-O, dry
7 c. Croc-O Berry Crunch cereal

Heat butter and marshmallows, stirring until melted. Remove from heat. Stir in gelatin. Quickly add cereal, stirring until all pieces are evenly coated. Press into a buttered 13" x 9" x 2" pan with a buttered spoon. Cool. Cut into squares.

204 *Wooden Spoon Wedding Cookbook*

CHOCOLATE OAT SCOTTIES

$^2/_3$ c. butter
1 c. packed brown sugar
$^1/_4$ c. corn syrup
$^1/_4$ c. plus $^2/_3$ c. chunky peanut
    butter, divided

1 t. vanilla
4 c. rolled oats
11$^1/_2$ oz. chocolate chips
$^1/_2$ c. butterscotch chips
1 c. salted peanuts

Melt the butter; stir in brown sugar and corn syrup until sugar is dissolved. Stir in $^1/_4$ c. peanut butter and vanilla until well blended. Add the oats; mix well. Press into a greased 13" x 9" baking pan. Bake at 375° for 12-15 minutes. Meanwhile, melt the chips and remaining peanut butter; stir in peanuts. Spread over crust. Refrigerate until cool. Cut into bars.

CHERRY MASH

5 (10 oz.) jars maraschino cherries   chocolate
5 (7 oz.) jars marshmallow creme
8 or 9 dippers (8 oz.) melted white coating

Drain and chop cherries. Mix well with marshmallow creme. Add melted white coating. Mix well and spread on layer of chocolate. Let cool and spread chocolate on top. Yield: 15-17 lb.

Mrs. Aden (Dora) Miller

SUGARLESS CANDY

1 c. ground raisins
1 c. peanut butter
$^1/_2$ c. nuts

2 c. Rice Krispies
2 lb. coating chocolate

Mix first 4 ingredients together and roll into balls. Dip in chocolate.

Mrs. Atlee V. (Barbara) Wengerd

He is a good friend, who says good things behind my back.

PIONEER FRUIT CANDY

1 lb. raisins	1 c. stoned prunes
$^1/_2$ lb. dates	juice and whole rind of oranges
$^1/_2$ lb. figs	1 c. walnuts

Grind together fruits and orange rind. Blend thoroughly with orange juice and nuts. Shape into bite-sized balls which can be rolled in coconut. Allow to stand 24 hours to ripen.

Mrs. Raymond B. (Iva) Miller

PERFECT PEPPERMINT PATTIES

1 box confectioner's sugar	$^1/_4$ c. evaporated milk
3 T. butter, softened	2 c. (12 oz.) semisweet chocolate
2-3 t. peppermint extract	chips
$^1/_2$ t. vanilla extract	2 T. shortening

In a bowl, combine first 4 ingredients. Add milk and mix well. Roll into 1" balls and place on a wax paper lined cookie sheet. Chill for 20 minutes. Flatten with a glass to $^1/_4$" thick. Chill for 30 minutes. In a double boiler, melt chocolate chips and shortening. Dip patties; place on waxed paper to harden. Yield: approximately 5 dozen.

Mrs. Ervin (Mary) Byler

PEANUT BRITTLE

2 c. sugar
1 c. water
1 c. King syrup
1¹/₂ c. blanched peanuts

1 t. butter
1 t. vanilla
2 t. baking soda

Cook sugar, water and syrup until hard ball forms in cold water or it threads (soft ball on candy thermometer). Add peanuts, butter and vanilla. Cook until golden brown (soft crack). Stir occasionally. Add baking soda. Stir well and pour quickly into buttered pans. Break in pieces when cool.

Mrs. Ervin (Mary) Byler

PEANUT BUTTER BALLS

1¹/₃ stick margarine
1¹/₂ c. peanut butter

3³/₄ c. powdered sugar
1 t. vanilla

Melt margarine; while still warm add peanut butter, powdered sugar and vanilla. Mix and form into small balls. Chill at least 1¹/₂ hours. Insert a toothpick into each ball and dip into chocolate, leaving a small bare space around toothpicks. Yield: approximately 65 balls.

Mrs. Ben D.A. (Fannie) Miller

FUDGY BUTTONS

4 T. butter
1 T. cocoa
1 c. powdered sugar

1 t. milk
¼ c. creamy peanut butter

In a small saucepan, melt butter; remove from heat. Add cocoa and mix well. Stir in powdered sugar; add milk and stir until smooth. Add peanut butter and mix well. Drop by teaspoonful onto waxed paper; flatten tops and shape into 1" patties.

Love makes everything lovely; hate concentrates itself on the one hated.

Wooden Spoon Wedding Cookbook

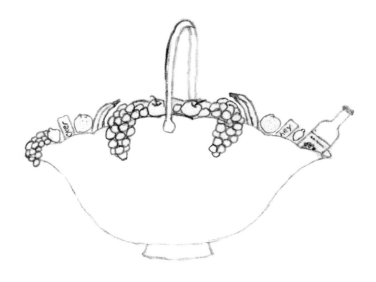

Aden gave me a glass basket as an Easter gift. I borrowed a matching one to use in the "eck." The baskets were filled with a bottle of sparkling grape juice, candy bars and fruit. The grape juice was enjoyed while washing dishes the day after the wedding, and the witnesses got to take the fruit and candy along home.

SOFT PRETZELS

4 t. yeast
$^1/_2$ t. salt
2 T. brown sugar

$1^1/_2$ c. warm water
1 T. oil
approximately $4^1/_2$ c. flour

Knead like you would bread dough. Let rise until double and then roll into pretzels any size you wish. Dip pretzels into a mixture of 2 t. soda and 1 c. warm water. Sprinkle with pretzel salt. Bake at 500° for approximately 10 minutes. Dip into melted butter and eat as soon as you can. Delicious with a glass of ice-cold lemonade.

Mrs. Mahlon (Katie) Miller

SOFT PRETZELS

$2^1/_2$ c. warm water
3 T. yeast
$^3/_4$ c. brown sugar

1 t. salt
7-8 c. bread flour

Let rise until double. Cut into strips and form, then dip in soda water (2 T. soda to 1 c. water). Place on well-greased cookie sheet and sprinkle with pretzel salt. Bake at 425° until brown, then dip in melted butter. Also good to roll in powdered sugar or cinnamon sugar after dipping in melted butter instead of putting on pretzel salt.

Ella L. Miller

tips and hints

COUNT YOUR AGE BY FRIENDS, NOT YEARS;
COUNT YOUR LIFE BY SMILES, NOT TEARS!

MRS. HENRY (ALMA) MAST

MINIATURE BIG MACS

vanilla wafer cookies

coconut

frosting

mint patties

Add green food coloring to the coconut and red food coloring to the frosting. The cookie looks like a hamburger bun. Spread red frosting on one cookie, as the ketchup; put the mint pattie on top as the hamburger. Add green coconut for the lettuce and top with another cookie with enough frosting to hold it together.

When I was in 7th or 8th grade, each week one family had to bring a finger food along to school for an afternoon snack. The snack had to start with the same letter as our mother's name. Since my mother's name is Mary we took Miniature Big Macs. The evening before we took them to school, we took our stuff up to Grandpas to make them, as they enjoyed watching.

CHRISTMAS EVE MICE

24 cream-filled chocolate
  sandwich cookies
1 c. semisweet chocolate chips
2 t. shortening
24 red maraschino cherries with
  stems, well drained

24 milk chocolate kisses
48 sliced almonds
1 small tube green decorative
  icing gel

Carefully twist cookies apart; set aside the halves with cream filling. Save
plain halves for another use. In a microwave or heavy saucepan, melt
chocolate chips and shortening; stir until smooth. Holding each cherry by
the stem, dip in melted chocolate, then press onto the bottom of a chocolate kiss. Place on the cream filling of cookies, with cherry stem extending
beyond cookie edge. For ears, place slivered almonds between the cherry
and kiss. Refrigerate until set. With green gel, pipe holly leaves on the
cream. With red gel, pipe berries between leaves and pipe eyes on each
chocolate kiss. Store in an airtight container at room temperature.

Elmina Miller

BIRTHDAY GIFT IDEAS

Mr./Mrs. WHATCHAMACALLIT,
We were going to give you 100 GRAND, but the money slipped through
our BUTTERFINGERS and we couldn't wait until PAYDAY, so we
looked on FIFTH AVENUE and found a trip to MARS and the MILKY
WAY, but neither seemed appropriate.
We wish you MOUNDS of ALMOND JOY as you CRUNCH through
another year.

Sincerely,
MR. GOOD BAR
THE 3 MUSKETEERS
BABY RUTH

P.S. We promise not to SNICKER at your age.

On a large piece of cardboard, print this birthday message, using candy
bars to complete the message.

Barbara Miller

PUDDINGWICHES

1¹/₂ c. cold milk
1 (3.9 oz.) pkg. chocolate
   instant pudding

¹/₄-¹/₂ c. peanut butter
15 whole graham crackers

Combine milk, instant pudding and peanut butter. Let stand for 5 minutes.
Break graham crackers in half. Spread pudding mixture over half of crackers; top with the remaining crackers. Wrap and freeze until firm. May be
frozen for up to 1 month.

I have a hummingbird collection. I collect anything with hummingbirds and this is my favorite piece. A friend carved the flowers and the hummingbird from wood. The base is a root.

PEANUTTY POPS

1 envelope unflavored gelatin
1 c. cold water
$^1/_2$ c. sugar

1 c. creamy peanut butter
1 c. chocolate milk

In a small saucepan, sprinkle gelatin over cold water; let stand for 1 minute. Stir in sugar; cook and stir over medium heat until gelatin and sugar are dissolved. Transfer to a mixing bowl. Beat in peanut butter and milk. Pour into popsicle cups and freeze.

POPSICLES

3 oz. Jell-O
1 envelope Kool-Aid
1 c. white sugar

2 c. hot water
2 c. cold water

Mix Jell-O and hot water until Jell-O is dissolved. Add cold water, sugar and Kool-Aid. Pour into popsicle trays.

Since we don't have refrigerators, this is a winter treat for us. As soon as the temperature drops low enough, out comes the popsicle recipe. Sometimes for a joke one of us would fill one of the popsicle cups with water and food coloring. What a tasteless popsicle!

PIGS IN A BLANKET

1 ('/₄ oz.) pkg. yeast	2 T. plus 2 t. shortening, melted
'/₃ c. plus 1 t. sugar, divided	1 t. salt
²/₃ c. warm milk (110° to 115°)	3²/₃ c. flour
'/₃ c. warm water (110° to 115°)	10 hot dogs
1 egg, beaten	2 slices process American cheese

Dissolve yeast and 1 t. sugar in milk and water; let stand 5 minutes. Add egg, shortening, salt, remaining sugar and enough flour to form a soft dough. Turn onto a floured surface; knead until smooth, approximately 8-10 minutes. Place in greased bowl; cover and let rise in a warm place until doubled, about 1 hour. Cut a '/₄" deep lengthwise slit in each hot dog. Cut cheese slices into five strips; place one strip in the slit of each hot dog. Punch dough down into a 5" x 2'/₂" rectangle and wrap around prepared hot dogs; pinch seam and ends to seal. Place seam down on greased baking sheets; let rise for 30 minutes. Bake at 350° for 15-18 minutes or until golden brown.

NOTES

Canning Freezing

Summer is a busy time of the year;
Sometimes almost too busy, I fear.
For then canning season is in full swing;
Lots of hard work it will bring!

There's plenty of strawberries to do,
And now there's peas and beans too.
The peaches and corn are ready the same day,
And so I can see no other way.

A husband so willing and kind,
Will surely get me out of my bind.
The jars are all filled, so to the shelves they go;
So nice and straight, we'll put them in a row.

Come winter we'll have plenty to eat,
As home-canned food can't be beat.
Many a child from hunger will cry;
For food we thank our Father on high!

I was not quite satisfied with just the usual menu for our wedding, and decided to have applesauce for supper since Aden is very fond of applesauce. It made a lot of people talk, but it was our wedding day and we enjoyed it right down to the applesauce!

CATSUP

4 qt. tomato juice	$^1/_2$ t. red pepper
3 c. sugar	$1^1/_2$ onion
2 T. salt	1 T. cinnamon
$^3/_4$ c. vinegar	1 t. ground mustard
1 T. pickled spice	

Put the last five ingredients in a small bag and remove after it's boiled. Boil everything together for 50 minutes. Add 4 T. Therm-Flo moistened with vinegar. Boil 10 minutes. Put in jars and seal.

Emma Miller

CHICKEN NOODLE SOUP

4 chickens	2 qt. potatoes
16 oz. noodles	6-7 qt. water for broth
2 qt. carrots	salt and chicken base to taste
1 qt. celery	

Cook chicken and add plenty of water for broth. Cook noodles and vegetables. Pressure cook quarts $1^1/_2$ hours; pints $1^1/_4$ hours.

Mrs. Jonas D.A. (Edna) Miller

tips and hints

WASH FRESH PINEAPPLE THOROUGHLY BEFORE
PARING. COVER PARINGS WITH WATER AND COOK
UNTIL SOFT. USE STRAINED JUICE TO MAKE JELLY

EMMA MILLER

CHEESEBURGER SOUP

10 lb. hamburger
4^1/$_2$ c. chopped onions
4^1/$_2$ c. cubed carrots
4^1/$_2$ c. cut up celery
4^1/$_2$ T. salt
3 t. pepper

3 t. basil
6 t. parsley
3 T. butter
24 c. chicken broth
24 c. cubed potatoes
2^1/$_2$ T. chicken base

Mix everything together and cold pack 3 hours. When opening, brown 2
T. butter and add 1 qt. milk to 1 pt. of this canned mixture. Thicken with
flour and add Velveeta cheese if desired.

Mrs. John (Susan) Miller

VEGETABLE SOUP

5 qt. tomato juice
2 qt. beef broth
1 pkg. sloppy joe seasoning
1 pkg. meat loaf seasoning
2 pkg. beef stew seasoning
2-3 lb. hamburger, fried

1 qt. each: potatoes, carrots, celery
    corn, peas, green beans
2 c. onions, chopped
1 large can pork and beans
1 box ABC macaroni
1 c. sugar

Combine tomato juice, beef broth, seasonings and sugar. Cook potatoes,
celery, carrots and macaroni. Fry hamburger. Combine all ingredients; add
salt and pepper to taste. Put in jars and cold pack 3 hours, or pressure cook
45 minutes. Yield: 16-17 quarts.

CHILI SOUP

15 lb. hamburger	**$^1/_3$ c. salt**
4 onions	**$1^1/_2$ c. brown sugar**
9 qt. tomato juice	**$1^1/_2$ c. white sugar**
9 qt. water	**2 pt. homemade ketchup**
4 (16 oz.) cans pork & beans	**2 qt. store-bought ketchup**
2 (16 oz.) cans baked beans	**1 c. Hunt's original BBQ sauce**
5 pkg. chili seasoning	

Brown hamburger and onions. Divide ingredients in 2 canners. To each canner add 2 T. chili powder and 1 t. each of onion, garlic and celery salts. Thicken with $1^1/_4$ c. clear jel in each canner. Pressure cook 1 hour at 10 lb. pressure. Yield: approximately 30 quarts. I usually add some water when I open it.

Mrs. Levi (Mary) Miller

COLD PACK SAUSAGE (SMOKED)

1 gal. water	**$^1/_2$ c. salt**
1 c. brown sugar	**1 T. pepper**

Cut sausage and put raw in jars. Fill jar with brine. Cold pack 30 minutes. Note: For unsmoked sausage cold pack 3 hours.

Before I got married we always had smoked sausage. Aden likes the un-smoked sausage better, so the first winter we were married I canned some the way he likes it. Only about half of the cans sealed. And the rest didn't keep either. I asked my mother-in-law about it. She said unsmoked sausage needs to be boiled 3 hours instead of only 30 minutes. The next time I remembered!

Those who labor not in love, labor in vain.

HOMEMADE BOLOGNA

$^1/_2$ lb. brown sugar
2 lb. Tenderquick
1$^1/_2$ oz. black pepper
$^1/_2$ oz. saltpeter
$^3/_4$ oz. garlic salt

1 lb. soda crackers
$^1/_2$ gal. milk
4 t. liquid smoke, or more if
  desired

Add above ingredients to 50 lb. ground meat. We like to add 10 lb. unseasoned ground pork or 5 lb. bacon. Grind bacon along with meat. Pack in jars and cold pack 3 hours or pressure cook 1$^1/_2$ hours at 10 lb. pressure.

Mrs. Jacob (Esther) Miller

HAMBURGER TO CAN

25 lb. hamburger
$^1/_2$ c. brown sugar
$^3/_4$ oz. black pepper

7 oz. salt
1 lb. crackers, crushed
$^1/_2$ gal. milk

Use hands to mix together. Stuff in jars. Pressure cook 90 minutes or cold pack 3 hours. This slices nicer than just the hamburger stuffed in jars. We like to fry it to go with a meal or slice it for cold sandwiches. No need to always have bought sandwich meat on hand.

GROUND CHICKEN MEAT

25 lb. ground chicken meat
$^3/_4$ c. salt
$^3/_4$ oz. black pepper
4 oz. brown sugar
$^1/_2$ lb. soda crackers, crushed

$^1/_2$ lb. rolled oats
1 qt. milk
1 qt. water
1 T. garlic powder
2 T. liquid smoke

Mix all together then put in cans. Pressure cook 1 hour.

Mrs. Emanuel R. (Fannie) Coblentz

VARIETY SAUCE

1 gal. tomato juice	1 t. cinnamon
2 T. salt	1 t. dry mustard
3 c. white sugar	$^1/_2$ t. red pepper
3 large onions, chopped	3 red or green peppers, chopped
1$^1/_2$ c. vinegar	

Mix together. Cook 1 hour, then add 6 T. cornstarch. Cook 10 minutes longer. Put in jars and seal. Good to use in sloppy joe or soups and casseroles.

Mrs. Uriah (Sevilla) Yoder

HEINZ CATSUP

1 peck tomatoes	1 T. salt
2 small peppers	$^1/_2$ t. dry mustard
3 large onions	1 pt. vinegar
4 c. white sugar	1 large can tomato paste
$^1/_2$ t. cloves	¼ c. cornstarch
$^1/_2$ t. cinnamon	

Boil tomatoes, peppers and onions together until soft and drain in jelly bag. Then put through Victorio strainer. Add next six ingredients and boil 10 minutes. Then add tomato paste and cornstarch.

Mrs. Eli (Ella) Stutzman

Wooden Spoon Wedding Cookbook   223

SLOPPY JOE SAUCE

12 large ripe tomatoes	1 t. cloves
1 red pepper	1 t. cinnamon
4 medium-sized apples	1 t. allspice
4 onions	3 c. vinegar, scant
2 T. salt	3 c. white sugar

Boil tomatoes, pepper, apples and onions until tender. Put through Victorio strainer, then put back on stove and add rest of ingredients. Boil until thick like ketchup. Have boiling hot to put in jars; seal. When ready to use add enough rolled oats or flour to fried hamburger to thicken. Stir; add sauce.

SALSA

3 gal. tomato juice	1 T. paprika
1 c. brown sugar	2 T. oregano
4 t. red pepper	1/2 c. salt
1 T. chili powder	1/2 t. celery seed
1 T. black pepper	

Boil together for 30 minutes.

Add:	**10 peppers**
2 c. clear jel	**8 onions**

Cool pack for 10 minutes.

When opening a jar we like to add shredded cheese to make a good chip dip. I use several hot peppers instead of sweet peppers. When making pizza I use half salsa and half pizza sauce.

TACO SALSA

20 large tomatoes or 40 Roma tomatoes	1 t. garlic salt
	2 c. white sugar
4 large onions	1 t. black pepper
4 carrots, grated	3 T. basil
3 green peppers	2 T. salt
5 hot peppers	1 t. cumin
8 jalapeñō peppers (4 with seeds)	1 T. lemon juice
1/2 c. parsley	1 (12 oz.) can tomato paste

Cut up vegetables with knife to get them chunky. Grate carrots. Cook slowly for 2 hours on top of stove. Add 1 T. lemon juice on top of each jar. Cold pack for at least 35 minutes. Good on top of eggs, toasted cheese or as a dip for nacho chips. Yield: approximately 12 pints.

Mrs. Levi (Mary) Miller

MIXED PICKLE

2 qt. lima beans	6 green peppers
1 qt. kidney beans	2 heads cauliflower
1 qt. finely cubed carrots	1 qt. cooked shell macaroni
1 qt. finely cubed celery	2 qt. small cucumbers
6 red peppers	1 qt. small onions

Cook all separately in water; add salt. Do not overcook. Cool.

Brine:

10 c. white sugar	4 t. celery seed
4 c. vinegar	2 T. turmeric
8 c. water	2 T. clear jel
1 t. cinnamon	

Mix brine. Heat to boiling. Then pour over vegetables. Put in jars and cold pack 1/2 hour.

Mrs. Crist (Verba) Miller

A great marriage is not when the "perfect couple" comes together. It is when an imperfect couple learns to enjoy their differences.

Wooden Spoon Wedding Cookbook **225**

LIME PICKLES

First Day:

7 lbs. cucumbers, unpeeled and
   sliced into 1" chunks or thinner,
   if desired

2 c. lime
2 gal. cold water

Second Day:

9 c. sugar
1 t. mixed spices
1 qt. vinegar
1 T. salt

1 T. celery seed
1 T. whole cloves
1 qt. water

Mix lime and water and pour over the cucumbers. Let stand 24 hours.
Wash out lime thoroughly. Cover with the sugar, vinegar, salt, water and
spice mixture. Do not heat. The next morning simmer the cucumbers 40
minutes. Put in hot jars and seal. These stay good and crisp. Less sugar
may be used. I put the spices in a little bag to put them with the pickles.

Mrs. Andy (Lizzie) Miller

tips and hints

ADD A LITTLE SALT TO APPLESAUCE; IT TAKES LESS

SUGAR AND BRINGS OUT A RICHER FLAVOR.

MRS. JOHN (KATIE) MILLER

ONION DILL PICKLES

1¹/₂ c. vinegar
3 c. water
3 c. sugar

2 T. salt
onions
dill heads

Slice pickles and fill to neck of jar. Add 1 onion slice and 1 head of dill to each jar. Heat other ingredients and fill jars. Put hot water in canner and cold pack only till boiling. Yield: 4 quarts.

This is our favorite pickle recipe, and very simple to can. Dill seed can be used instead of a dill head, but to me it's much better with the dill heads. Mom planted dill in the garden when I was still at home. It kept coming up every year and spreading. To me that looked like an untidy garden with dill growing between the rows. So one spring when the first plants came up I pulled them before Mom could tell me not to, thinking there would be plenty more coming up. My punishment was pickles with only dill seed that year, as I had pulled every plant that came up. Mom actually thought it was funny, since I'm the main dill pickle eater in the family. And now Cristy likes them as well as I do.

Aden & Miriam

GARLIC DILL PICKLES

3 c. sugar
2 c. water
2 c. vinegar

2 T. salt
1 t. dill seed
¹/₄ t. garlic powder

Bring the first 4 ingredients to a boil. Fill jars with sliced cucumbers. Add dill seed and garlic powder. Add hot syrup and seal. Put in hot water bath; bring to a boil. Immediately remove from hot water. Ready to eat in 2 weeks. Yield: 4 quarts.

Mrs. Ervin (Mary) Miller

Wooden Spoon Wedding Cookbook   **227**

BLUEBERRIES TO CAN

4 qt. water
5 c. sugar

3¹/₂ qt. blueberries

Mix water and sugar; add 1 qt. blueberries. Bring to a boil. Add the rest of
the blueberries and bring to a boil again. When boiling again, thicken with
Perma-Flo to your liking. Put in jars and seal. I like to have some thick
enough for puddings and pie fillings and some only slightly thickened to
eat as fruit.

Ever heard of the saying, "Many hands make light work"? It's true! Aden's
parents have several blueberry bushes and more blueberries than they can
eat. So I said I want some that week, but I was wondering, "How will I find
time to can them?" My week looked busy already. So one evening after
supper Aden's four youngest sisters came with the blueberries—and
willing hands. Almost before I knew what was happening, they
started to can them. In less than two hours I had 16 qt. blueberries in jars and the dishes all washed!

PEACH PIE FILLING

6 qt. sliced peaches
3 c. pineapple juice
3 c. water

7 c. sugar
2 small boxes apricot Jell-O
2 c. Perma-Flo

Boil water, juice and sugar together. Then mix 2 c. Perma-Flo with 1¹/₂ c.
water. Add this to the boiling mixture. Cook; stir until thick; add Jell-O,
then add peaches last. Put in jars; cold pack for 20 minutes.

Mrs. Jonas D.A. (Edna) Miller

PEACH MARMALADE

5 c. crushed peaches
5 c. sugar
1 (15 oz.) can crushed pineapple

6 oz. orange, strawberry or
    pineapple Jell-O

Cook peaches, sugar and crushed pineapple together for 15 minutes. Add Jell-O. Cook until dissolved. Pour in jars and seal.

Mrs. Alvin (Ida) Miller

RHUBARB-RASPBERRY JAM

5 c. chopped rhubarb
4 c. white sugar

12 oz. raspberry juice
3 oz. raspberry Jell-O

In a large bowl, combine rhubarb, sugar and raspberry juice. Refrigerate 5 hours. Place rhubarb mixture in a large saucepan and bring to a boil. Simmer 10 minutes, stirring often. Remove from heat. Add Jell-O. Put in jars and cold pack 5 minutes. Yield: 3 pints.

Emma Miller

RHUBARB-CHERRY JAM

6 c. rhubarb, finely diced
1 T. butter
21 oz. cherry pie filling

4 c. sugar
3 oz. cherry Jell-O

Mix rhubarb and sugar in a large saucepan. Let set overnight. Add butter and cook 10 minutes. Add Jell-O and pie filling and cook for one minute.

A successful partnership consists not only of those things spoken, but those things left unspoken. Loyalty is what we seek in friendship.

Wooden Spoon Wedding Cookbook   **229**

The spring before our wedding we had more strawberries than we could eat. Our kind neighbor let us put them in his freezer, and that way we had them for the wedding. We chopped them and added sugar before we froze them. That way they were ready to thaw and enjoy the day of the wedding.

SWEET CORN TO FREEZE

12 c. raw sweet corn
$^1/_2$ c. butter
1 t. salt

$^1/_2$ c. sugar
$^3/_4$ c. milk

Combine all ingredients and cook until it boils, stirring often. Cool, box and freeze. When ready to use, heat in double boiler until hot.

Mrs. Ben D.A. (Fannie) Miller

CANNED SLEEP

$^1/_2$ doz. naps
40 winks

$^1/_2$ c. energy

Mix together and put in pint jars. Fill with water. Cook for 10 minutes. Best when served Monday morning, right out of the jars.

tips and hints

WHEN BLACKBERRIES ARE IN SEASON FILL A PINT JAR
HALFWAY WITH BLACKBERRIES THEN FILL JAR WITH
WHITE SUGAR. ALLOW TO STAND IN COOL PLACE TILL
CONTENTS ARE LIQUIFIED. TAKE TWO TABLESPOONS
FOR UPSET STOMACH.

NOTES

Miscellaneous

It's rather hard to write a poem for this section,
As there are many recipes to be found.
If you couldn't find the recipe elsewhere,
It's sure to be in this section if you look around.

For there's Danish Dessert and marshmallow creme,
Also yogurt and goat milk cheese.
Taco seasoning, pancake syrup,
Apple fritters and lollipops, if you please!

If you love to watch the birds,
Make some suet with peanut butter.
They sure seem to enjoy it,
And I love to see them flutter.

And if you are like most everyone else,
You've got some weeds that you'd like to kill.
If you look through this book,
You can make your own killer, without a bill.

MISCELLANEOUS

YOGURT WITH GOAT MILK

2 qt. milk	**³/₄ c. white sugar**
2 T. gelatin	**2 T. active yogurt**
¹/₂ c. water	

Heat milk to 190°. Remove from heat and cool to 130°. Now add gelatin soaked in cold water, white sugar and active yogurt. Beat with wire whisk. Cover and let set for 3-4 hours. Stir well. If you want it flavored, add fruit thickened with clear jel—the amount you want. Pour into containers. Let cool at room temperature until completely cooled. Refrigerate.

Mrs. Ivan A. Miller

GOAT MILK CHEESE

1 gal. fresh cold milk	**2 egg yolks, beaten**
³/₄ c. vinegar	**¹/₂ c. milk**
1 t. soda	**1 t. salt**
¹/₃ c. butter	

Heat milk to 160°. Remove from heat and add vinegar. Stir, then let set uncovered until cool. Strain through a cloth and hang up for 3-4 hours to drain. Crumble with fork and add soda. Let set 30 minutes. On VERY LOW heat melt butter and add the cheese crumbles. After cheese is smooth, add beaten egg yolks, milk and salt. Heat to almost boiling. Add a few slices Velveeta cheese if desired.

Mrs. Ivan A. Miller

tips and hints

TO GET COLOR MARKS OFF THE WALL, RUB WITH

TOOTHPASTE BEFORE WASHING.

HAM GLAZE

4 c. pineapple juice
5$^{1}/_{4}$ c. brown sugar

4 t. dry mustard
3 T. clear jel

Mix pineapple juice and brown sugar. Bring to a boil. Add enough water to clear jel to make a paste. Add to first mixture. Last, mix water and mustard to make a paste. Add to glaze. This is enough glaze for 10 lb. ham, sliced $^{1}/_{4}$" thick.

Mrs. Dan (Emma) Miller

CINNAMON BUTTER

$^{3}/_{4}$ lb. Country Crock
1 c. powdered sugar

1 t. cinnamon

Mix together. Refrigerate a few hours, then you need to work this like you do homemade butter.

Mrs. John (Susan) Miller

WHITE SUGAR SPREAD FOR BREAD

2 c. white sugar
2 c. brown sugar

4 c. light Karo
1 t. vanilla

Boil 2 minutes. When cool, but not cold, add 5 egg whites, beaten stiff, and stir until cold. The more you stir the fluffier it gets.

Mrs. Dan (Emma) Miller

GRAPE MOLASSES

1 pt. grape juice
3 lb. white sugar

1 pt. light Karo

Boil scant three minutes. Any fruit juice can be used to make this jam.

Mrs. Leroy (Katie) Miller

MISCELLANEOUS

DANISH DESSERT

$^1/_3$ c. white sugar

2 T. clear jel or Perma-Flo

$^1/_4$ c. Jell-O, any flavor

2 c. water

Mix dry ingredients and water. Bring to a boil. Add sliced fruit of your choice. This is the right amount for one pie.

DANISH FOR FRUIT PIES

3 c. water

1 c. sugar

6 T. clear jel

$1^1/_2$ c. cold water

$^3/_4$ c. Jell-O

Dissolve clear jel in $1^1/_2$ c. cold water. Mix 3 c. water and sugar; add clear jel mixture. Bring to a boil; boil for 3 minutes. Take off heat and add Jell-O (flavor of pie). If too thick when ready to serve, add water.

APPLE FRITTERS

1 c. flour

3 T. white sugar

$1^1/_2$ t. baking powder

$^1/_4$ t. salt

$^1/_2$ c. milk

1 egg

2 or 3 apples, sliced

Mix first four ingredients. Add milk and egg. Last add apples. Drop in hot oil by spoonsful until browned. Dip in pancake syrup.

Mrs. Dan (Emma) Miller

236 *Wooden Spoon Wedding Cookbook*

MISCELLANEOUS

LOLLIPOPS

Sugar Mixture:

$^{1}/_{4}$ t. nutmeg

$^{1}/_{2}$ t. cinnamon

$^{1}/_{2}$ c. brown sugar

$^{1}/_{2}$ c. white sugar

Syrup:

1 c. brown sugar

1 c. water

Take bread dough and shape into small balls. Roll in butter then in sugar mixture. Put in a pan and pour syrup over it. Bake until lollipops are done. Serve warm with milk.

Verba Miller

TACO SEASONING

2 T. chili powder

5 t. paprika

$4^{1}/_{2}$ t. ground cumin

3 t. onion powder

3 t. salt

$2^{1}/_{2}$ t. garlic powder

$^{1}/_{8}$ t. cayenne pepper

Combine all ingredients and store in airtight container. Tastes almost like store-bought.

BABY WIPES

2 c. boiling water

3 T. baby bath

1 T. baby oil

Cut a roll of Bounty towels in half. Place upright in an airtight container and pour solution over it. Remove center cardboard. Cover tightly and it's ready to use in 1 hour. The wipes can be pulled up from the center just like the store-bought ones.

MARSHMALLOW CREME

2 c. white sugar
2³/₄ c. light Karo, divided

1 c. water
⁷/₈ c. egg whites

Mix sugar, 2¹/₂ c. Karo and water in a 3 quart saucepan. Cook to 240°. While cooking beat ¹/₄ c. Karo and egg whites until very stiff. Slowly pour cooked mixture over stiffly beaten egg whites and beat slowly. When mixed, beat for several minutes, then use spoon and stir often. When cold, store in glass jars. Add some of your favorite jam or jelly—delicious on bread, or use in fruit dips, etc. Almost same as store-bought.

CRUNCHY CHOCOLATE SAUCE

1 c. chopped walnuts or pecans
¹/₂ c. butter (no substitutes)

1 (6 oz.) pkg. chocolate chips

In a skillet, sauté nuts in butter until golden. Remove from heat; stir in chocolate chips until melted. Serve warm over ice cream. Leftovers can be reheated. This sauce is like the Magic Shell topping that can be bought. It hardens when it is put on ice cream. Even people who don't care for nuts like this as they are so crisp, almost like Rice Krispies.

BUTTERSCOTCH SAUCE FOR ICE CREAM

³/₄ c. brown sugar
2 T. butter
pinch of salt

¹/₂ c. light corn syrup
¹/₃ c. light cream

Place everything in saucepan except cream. Cook until soft ball stage or until a soft ball when tested in cold water. Cool slightly. Stir in cream. If it gets too thick while cooling, add 1-2 T. milk or cream. Yield: approximately 1¹/₄ cups.

Mrs. Jacob D. (Esther) Miller

FLANNEL PANCAKES

2 c. flour	4 t. baking powder
2 T. brown sugar	2 eggs, beaten
1 T. melted butter	$^1/_4$ t. salt

Mix together. Add enough sweet milk to make a fairly thin batter. Fry in hot griddle with a little vegetable oil.

Mrs. Leroy (Katie) Miller

PANCAKE SYRUP

3 c. brown sugar	$1^1/_2$ c. water
1 c. white sugar	1 T. maple flavoring
3 c. corn syrup	

Heat first 4 ingredients until sugar is dissolved, then add maple flavoring. Tastes like store-bought syrup.

PLAY DOUGH

1 c. flour	1 T. vegetable oil
1 c. water	2 t. cream of tartar
$^1/_2$ t. salt	food coloring

Mix dry ingredients together. Add vegetable oil and water. Blend liquid in slowly to form a smooth dough. Cook for approximately 3 minutes, or until mixture is all on one lump. Add food coloring and knead almost immediately into a smooth ball. Store in airtight container.

Fame is the scentless sunflower with gaudy crowns of gold, but friendship is the breathing rose with sweet in every fold.

Wooden Spoon Wedding Cookbook **239**

MISCELLANEOUS

PEANUT BUTTER SUET

1 c. lard (no substitute)
1 c. crunchy peanut butter
2 c. quick oats
2 c. cornmeal
1 c. flour
$\frac{1}{3}$ c. sugar

Melt lard and peanut butter. Add rest of ingredients. May add other ingredients like sunflower seeds or raisins.

This is a cheap way to feed the birds and they really seem to like it. If I have old lard, this is how I use it. The birds don't mind.

WEED KILLER

1 gal. white vinegar
3 c. salt
1 reg. size bottle detergent

Mix together and spray. Kills weeds on the spot. Works faster than Roundup.

Mrs. David (Anna) Miller

BLIGHT ON VEGETABLES

1 gal. water
1 T. saltpeter
1 T. Epsom salt
1 T. baking powder
1 T. ammonia
1 T. dishwashing detergent

In a 4 gallon bucket mix saltpeter and Epsom salt. Add a little warm water to dissolve salt. Add the rest of ingredients and cold water. Pour into sprinkling can and give each plant 1 pint every 2 weeks.

Mrs. Atlee V. (Barbara) Wengerd

Index

BEVERAGES

Holiday Punch.................................3
Hot Chocolate................................7
Iced Tea...6
Mennonite Wine 4
Punch..4
Punch..5
Punch..5
Quick Root Beer.............................6
Rhubarb Drink...............................6
Wedding Punch..............................4

BREADS, ROLLS, & CEREALS

Best Cinnamon Rolls 18
Biscuits 15
Biscuits A La Nancy.......................15
Brown -n- Serve Buns....................14
Brown Bread.................................13
Cereal...20
Cereal...21
Cinnamon Twists...........................20
Easy Buttermilk Biscuits 15
Granny Bread 11
Granola Cereal 21
Grape Nuts....................................22
Mom's Homemade Bread 11
Oatmeal Rolls 18
Quick Buns 10
Raspberry-cream Cheese Rolls 19
Rolls 17
Sour Cream Rolls 19
Sweet Potato Biscuits.....................17
Two-hour Buns 14

Uncooked Granola Cereal 21
White Bread 13

SALADS & SALAD DRESSINGS

Cauliflower Broccoli Salad 27
L&k Dressing.................................30
Potato Salad..................................27
Salad Dressing...............................30
Sweet -n- Sour Dressing.................31
Taco Salad.....................................25
Taco Salad.....................................28
Vegetable Pizza..............................26
Vegetable Pizza..............................28
Vegetable Pizza..............................29

MEATS & MAIN DISHES

3 Lb. Noodles................................64
Bacon Cheeseburger Casserole 57
Bacon Cheeseburger Rice..............58
Baked Onion Rings 67
Barbecued Meatballs 44
Beef Burger Pie 53
Bill's Sandwiches 46
Breakfast Casserole 41
Cheeseburger 'N Fries Casserole....53
Cheeseburger Pie 54
Chicken and Biscuits 60
Chicken and Biscuits 60
Chicken Burgers............................45
Chicken Casserole 61
Chicken Crumbs 40
Chicken Crumbs 43

Wooden Spoon Wedding Cookbook   **241**

INDEX

Chicken Gumbo 61
Chicken Pot Pie 59
Chicken Turnovers 46
Corn Dogs 48
Creamy Potato Sticks 49
Crispy Potato Wedges 52
Crunchy Potato Balls 52
Dandelion Gravy 66
Dressing (or Stuffing) 37
Dressing (or Stuffing) 63
Dumplings 65
Easy Wigglers 62
French Pizza 57
Fried Dill Pickle Coins 67
Fried Squash Blossoms 66
Gravy 36
Ham and Green Bean
     Casserole 63
Lasagna 58
Macaroni Ham Casserole 62
Maple French Toast 55
Mashed Potatoes 35
Meat Loaf 39
Meat Loaf 42
Meat Loaf 44
Mock Ham 45
Noodles for Wedding 43
Pizza 64
Pizza Casserole 56
Pizza Casserole 56
Potato and Egg Casserole 49
Potato Casserole 48
Potluck Potatoes 42
Quick and Easy Breakfast 54
Sauerkraut Casserole 59
Seasoned Fan Potatoes 51
Taco Shells 64
Tortilla Roll-ups 65
Yummi-Setti 38

Zesty Lemon Potatoes 51

SOUPS & VEGETABLES

Cabbage Chowder 75
Carrot Casserole 76
Cheddar Ham Soup 77
Cheeseburger Soup 70
Cheeseburger Soup 71
Cheeseburger Soup 71
Cheesy Chicken Chowder 75
Chili Soup 74
Chunky Chicken Soup (To Can) 73
Escalloped Corn 76
Mixed Vegetables 70
Onion Cheese Soup 74
Potato Soup 73

PIES

Apple Pie 80
Apple Pie 83
Blueberry Custard Pie 95
Chocolate Mocha Pie 89
Chocolate Pie 90
Coconut Oatmeal Pie 94
Creamy Pumpkin Pie 97
Custard Pie 95
Custard Pie 96
Fresh Pear Pie 84
Fresh Raspberry Pie 86
Imitation Pecan Pie 83
Lemon Meringue Pie 85
Magic Apple Pie 84
Mother's Special Pumpkin Pie 96
Mounds Pie 92
Oatmeal Pie 94
Peanut Butter Pie 81
Peanut Butter Pie 87

242   *Wooden Spoon Wedding Cookbook*

INDEX

Peanut Butter Pie 89
Pecan Pie 90
Pecan Pie 91
Raspberry Pie 86
Rhubarb Cream Pie 87
Rice Krispie Pie 91
Surprise Pecan Pie 82
Vanilla Crumb Pie 92

CAKES, COOKIES & FROSTINGS

4-layer Bars 130
Abe Mary Cookies 157
Angel Food Cake 102
Angel Food Cake 122
Angel Food Jelly Roll 123
Banana Cookies 146
Best Chocolate Chip Cookies 139
Blueberry Muffins 126
Brown Sugar Frosting 162
Brown Sugar Shortbread 136
Bushel Cookies 146
Buttercream Frosting 161
Butterscotch Cookies 149
Butterscotch Crunch
    Sandwich Cookies 150
Butterscotch Fudge Bars 131
Cake Mix Cookies 156
Can't Leave Alone Bars 134
Candy-topped Bars 131
Caramel Cake 108
Caramel Cookies 153
Checker Board Cake 119
Chewy Mocha Kisses 141
Chiffon Cake 103
Chocolate Chip Bars 134
Chocolate Chip Cookies 138
Chocolate Chip Sandwich
    Cookies 137

Chocolate Drop Cookies 140
Chocolate Frosting 161
Chocolate Marshmallow Bars 133
Chocolate Pinwheels 160
Coconut Oatmeal Cookies............145
Cowboy Coffee Cake 124
Cream-filled Coffee Cake 114
Cream-filled Coffee Cake 115
Cream Wafer Cookies 151
Cream Wafer Cookies 152
Crispy Cereal Meringues 160
Crumb Cake 124
Danny Emma Cookies...................153
Debbie Cookies 154
Disappearing Marshmallow
    Brownies 133
Double-decker Brownies 130
Dump Cake....................................118
Five-flavor Pound Cake 122
Fluffy White Cake 106
Fresh Apple Bars 129
Frosted Pumpkin Gems................127
Fudge Nut Bars..............................132
Fudgy Brownie Cookies................143
Ho-ho Cake 118
Jelly Roll..101
Jelly Roll..123
Lazy Wife Cake 105
Lazy Woman's Cake 106
Luscious Lemon Bars....................129
Maple Leaf Cookies.......................158
Mexican Chocolate Chiffon 102
Mini Coffee Cakes 126
Mississippi Mud Bars...................132
Mocha Walnut Cookies 141
Molasses Cake (Sugarless)............114
Mom's Soft Chocolate Chip
    Cookies 137

Wooden Spoon Wedding Cookbook   **243**

Index

Monster Cookies 159
Mule Ears 161
My Chocolate Cake 104
My Favorite Chocolate Cake 105
My True Love Cake 117
Oat Filled Cookies 144
Oatmeal Nut Cake 112
One-bowl Chocolate Cake 104
Peanut Butter Bars 135
Peanut Butter Cookies 148
Peanut Butter Cookies 148
Peanut Butter Dream Bars 135
Pie Crust Cookies 158
Pie Crust Cookies 159
Poppy Seed Chiffon Cake 111
Pumpkin Bars 127
Pumpkin Drop Cookies 147
Pumpkin Whoopie Pies 147
Rolled Oats Cookies 145
S'more Sandwich Cookies 143
Shortcake 125
Shortcake 125
Soft Batch Cookies 136
Sponge Cake 107
Sugar Cookies 152
Sugar Plum Spice Cake 112
Trilby Cookies 144
Triple-layer Mocha Cake 120
Triple Treat Cookies 149
Ultimate Chocolate Chip
    Cookies 138
Wedding Cake Frosting 103
Whoopie Pie Cookies 156
Zucchini Cake 108
Zucchini Squash Cake 109

Desserts & Pudding

Angel Food Cake Pudding 172

Apple Crisp 189
Apple Crisp 189
Apple Dumplings 181
Blueberry Buckle 187
Brown Betty 190
Brown Sugar Dumplings 191
Butterscotch Tapioca 176
Cherry Gelatin Salad 183
Chocolate Trifle 173
Cooked Apple Snitz 180
Corn Pone 190
Corn Pone 190
Cornstarch Pudding 191
Cracker-Cream Cheese
    Pudding 169
Cream Cheese Cracker
    Pudding 174
Crust Salad 166
Date Pudding 165
Date Pudding 170
Delicious Jell-o Mold 183
Danish Dessert 167
Florida Pudding 171
Fruit Cobbler 186
Fruit Salad 178
Graham Cracker Crust 173
Graham Cracker Pudding 174
Graham Cracker Pudding 175
Homemade Ice Cream 178
Hot Fudge Pudding 175
Ice Cream Salad 184
Indiana Salad 186
Layered Toffee Cake 172
Lime Delight 182
Lime Salad (Sugar-free) 182
Mallow Cream 177
Mandarin Orange Salad 184
Oreo Cookie Pudding 171
Peach Intrigue 191

244   *Wooden Spoon Wedding Cookbook*

INDEX

Pearl Tapioca With
    Cream Cheese 176
Pineapple Fluff 177
Pineapple Pretzel Fluff 177
Red and Green Gelatin 181
Rhubarb Torte 188
Ribbon Salad 183
Slush 180
Tropical Fruit Dessert 178
Wedding Date Pudding
    and Sauce 168

CANDIES & SNACKS

3-layer Keebler Bars 201
Birthday Gift Ideas 212
Butter Mints 194
Caramel Corn 196
Caramel Corn—fit For A King 196
Cherry Mash 205
Chocolate-covered Snack Mix 204
Chocolate Oat Scotties 205
Chocolate Peanut Butter
    Pebbles 204
Christmas Eve Mice 211
Christmas Wreath 203
Creamy Cheese Ball 203
Crispy Pretzel Bars 202
Crunchy Popcorn 195
Donut Holes 198
Fudgy Buttons 207
Granola Bars 200
Granola Bars 200
Hocky Pucks (Sugarless) 198
Hot Mustard Pretzel Dip 203
Miniature Big Macs 210
No-bake Bars 202
Party Mix 195
Patties 199

Peanut Brittle 207
Peanut Butter Balls 207
Peanutty Pops 214
Perfect Peppermint Patties 206
Pigs In A Blanket 215
Pioneer Fruit Candy 206
Popcorn Cake 196
Popsicles 214
Puddingwiches 212
Pull Buns 199
S'mores Bars 201
Soft Pretzels 209
Soft Pretzels 209
Strawberry Marshmallow
    Squares 204
Sugarless Candy 205

CANNING & FREEZING

Blueberries To Can 228
Canned Sleep 231
Catsup 219
Cheeseburger Soup 220
Chicken Noodle Soup 219
Chili Soup 221
Cold Pack Sausage (Smoked) 221
Garlic Dill Pickles 227
Ground Chicken Meat 222
Hamburger To Can 222
Heinz Catsup 223
Homemade Bologna 222
Lime Pickles 226
Mixed Pickle 225
Onion Dill Pickles 227
Peach Marmalade 229
Peach Pie Filling 228
Rhubarb-cherry Jam 229
Rhubarb-raspberry Jam 229

Wooden Spoon Wedding Cookbook   **245**

INDEX

Salsa 224
Sloppy Joe Sauce...........................224
Sweet Corn To Freeze 231
Taco Salsa 225
Variety Sauce...............................223
Vegetable Soup..............................220

MISCELLANEOUS

Apple Fritters 236
Baby Wipes.....................................237
Blight On Vegetables....................240
Butterscotch Sauce
    For Ice Cream 238
Cinnamon Butter 235
Crunchy Chocolate Sauce.............238

Danish Dessert..............................236
Danish For Fruit Pies...................236
Flannel Pancakes 239
Goat Milk Cheese...........................234
Grape Molasses 235
Ham Glaze 235
Lollipops..237
Marshmallow Creme 238
Pancake Syrup...............................239
Peanut Butter Suet 240
Play Dough 239
Taco Seasoning..............................237
Weed Killer.....................................240
White Sugar Spread For Bread.....235
Yogurt With Goat Milk.................234

Miriam's Wedding Recipes Index

BEVERAGES
Holiday Punch....................................3

BREADS, ROLLS & CEREALS
Quick Buns 10

SALADS & SALAD DRESSINGS
Taco Salad...25
Vegetable Pizza...............................26

MEATS & MAIN DISHES
Breakfast Casserole 41
Chicken Crumbs 40
Gravy 36
Dressing (or Stuffing) 37

Mashed Potatoes 35
Meat Loaf...39
Yummi-Setti 38

PIES
Apple Pie...80
Peanut Butter Pie 81
Surprise Pecan Pie 82

CAKES, COOKIES & FROSTINGS
Jelly Roll..101

DESSERTS & PUDDINGS
Crust Salad 166
Date Pudding 165
Danish Dessert 167

246   *Wooden Spoon Wedding Cookbook*